# PRAYE

## *A Biblical Perspective*

With warm gratitude
for fellowship ministry

Eric J. Alexander.

# PRAYER
## *A Biblical Perspective*

Eric J. Alexander

THE BANNER OF TRUTH TRUST

THE BANNER OF TRUTH TRUST
3 Murrayfield Road, Edinburgh EH12 6EL, UK
P.O. Box 621, Carlisle, PA 17013, USA

\*

© Eric J. Alexander 2012

\*

ISBN: 978 1 84871 149 5

\*

Typeset in 11/15 Adobe Caslon Pro at
the Banner of Truth Trust, Edinburgh

Printed in the U.S.A. by
Versa Press, Inc.,
East Peoria, IL

To

Jennifer and Ronald

# CONTENTS

# INTRODUCTION

ANYONE WHO SETS ABOUT WRITING a book on prayer inevitably does so with a great measure of diffidence, even reluctance. Having found this myself, I have tried to assess why it should be so, and I think the answer is twofold. First it is because prayer is an intensely personal area of one's life, and we all have a natural reluctance to speak or write about personal matters. The second reason is not unrelated to the first: it is because we all have a deep sense of inadequacy in this area of our Christian living, and a conviction that here above everywhere we have a far greater need to be taught than to teach. Before you begin to read this book, I would like to affirm that conviction for myself. I find prayer at one and the same time a great delight and a major challenge. I am reluctant to pray, and often find myself troubled by wandering thoughts when I do. But I am encouraged to find that so many greater men than I have found the same problems. Thomas Watson, the Puritan, confesses that 'Christ went more readily to the Cross than we do to the throne of grace'. Martin Luther complains that he is not so intent on the subject of his prayers as his dog is on its dinner!

But whatever the difficulties, there is no doubt that throughout the Bible, prayer is fundamental and not supplemental in the personal and corporate lives of God's people. Nowhere is this more exemplified than in the life and teaching of Jesus, and in the life and ministry of the apostolic church. That we need to learn this priority in our generation most urgently is demonstrated by the fact that none of us would have difficulty in answering the question 'Which is the least well attended meeting in my church?'. It is of course the prayer meeting. This can only be because we regard the ministry of prayer as supplemental rather than fundamental in the church of Jesus Christ. It is my most earnest desire that if this little book accomplishes anything, it may be a contribution to reversing this situation in the Christian church.

ERIC J. ALEXANDER
November 2011

# A BIOGRAPHICAL PROLOGUE
## ON KNOWING GOD

THE FIRST REAL CHRISTIAN I ever knew at close quarters was my brother. He was four years older than I and he had just completed his National Service. It would be difficult to imagine the scene at our family breakfast table one morning, when a letter arrived from my brother telling us that he had become a Christian while serving in the army.

I confess I was a bit apprehensive when he later returned home. We had been regular attenders at our local parish church, and I was under the impression that our whole family were Christians. I had prepared myself to receive some kind of religious maniac into the family. However, to my great surprise my brother scarcely spoke about his new-found faith; the transformation in his life was so complete and obvious that I was deeply curious about what it was exactly that had happened to him. His favourite way of describing it was to say that he had 'come to know God through Jesus'. How strange, for I thought that, having been through Sunday School and Bible Class, I knew a fair amount about God and Jesus.

Then one evening it struck me. My father asked my brother if, before going to bed, he would lead the family in prayer about an important decision which had to be made. After he had finished praying and left the room, I said to my parents, 'He speaks to God as though he really knows him.' My mother added, 'I think he does.'

One of my great difficulties, on the rare occasions when I tried to pray, was that I felt I was speaking to somebody I did not really know—a stranger. Could that, I wondered, be the simple truth?

In a later conversation, my brother pointed out to me that *knowing about God* was simply a matter of research, whereas *knowing God* was a matter of relationship. Knowing about God might eventually make you into a clever theologian but, according to the words of Jesus, it would not give you eternal life and make you a Christian.

In the Gospel of John (14:6), Jesus said, 'I am the way and the truth and the life. No one comes to the Father except through me. If you really knew me, you would know my Father as well.' I gradually began to realise that these words of Jesus, in John 17:3 and John 14:6, were telling me two things:

Firstly, they were telling me that there is only one God to know ('That they may know you, *the only true God*'). Thus Jesus did not believe in a plurality of gods. Of course there are many gods whom people worship, but they are false gods.

And secondly, that there is *only one way to know this God*, and that is through Jesus Christ, the person God sent into the world and in whom God makes himself known.

I had always believed that there were almost innumerable ways to God. But if that were true, then what Jesus said was untrue. There was no room for doubt about what Jesus had said. Neither was there room for doubt about what happened in my brother's life, which was now so redolent with truth and reality. Truth was what really mattered to him now, and for this reason he became a diligent student of the Bible. He was more balanced, sane, and clear-minded than I had ever known him. I deeply longed to have the same faith in Christ, the same reality in my relationship with God, and the same assurance of eternal life as my brother possessed and enjoyed. I frequently asked God to open my eyes that I too might come to know him. Within a few months, God had answered my plea, and I was drawn (it is the only word I can use) to know him, and to want to know him more and more.

I have been a Christian now for more than sixty years. If there is one thing I have learned which is perhaps more important than anything else, it is that knowing God is a progressive, growing experience and not something static. That is why Paul, with years of Christian experience behind him, could say in his letter to the Philippians, 'I want to know Christ' (*Phil.* 3:10). This is a feature that we all recognise in our human relationships. We may ask a friend, 'Do you know so and so?' and they may answer, 'Vaguely, but not personally', or 'We are in touch now and again', or 'Of course I know him, our relationship is close and deep and very precious to me.' You could use similar language to speak of our knowledge of God in Christ. The human parallel also gives the clue to what lies behind the depth of a relationship. A personal relationship deepens when we spend time in another's presence and when there is a flow of one mind and heart to another. Our knowledge of God grows and develops when he speaks to us and reveals himself to us in his Word (the Bible), and when we speak to him in prayer and praise.

When I was newly converted, I remember asking my brother, 'How can I learn to pray?' I remember his reply to this day. 'Why don't you try asking Jesus what his disciples asked him at the beginning of Luke 11, "Lord, teach us to pray."' Then he added, 'I'm sure there is nothing he would rather do.'

Why don't you pray the disciples' prayer before you read any further in this book?

# I

# WHAT IS PRAYER?

WE MUST BEGIN OUR THINKING by considering what 'prayer' is. Of course, to begin with some kind of definition is not a necessity exclusive to prayer; indeed it could be applied to almost every subject. But circumstances make the necessity more pressing in the twenty-first century. The fact is that few subjects are so much misunderstood, even in the evangelical Christian church at this time, as the subject of prayer. Therefore, it is an indispensable necessity to clarify what we mean by 'prayer from a biblical perspective'.

At the outset, we need to 'clear the ground' of some of the most common misunderstandings.

Firstly, prayer is not an alibi for doing nothing—a substitute for work. In my own experience, prayer is actually the hardest kind of work I have ever had to do. Indeed, in his excellent book on the subject of prayer, Professor Hallesby has an entire chapter on 'Prayer as Work'.[1]

Secondly, prayer is not simply or mainly 'asking God for things we need' as one prayer manual suggests. It is not just a means of obtaining favours from God. Indeed it is primarily worship and adoration of God for his greatness and grace.

Thirdly, prayer is not a mechanical recitation of a form of words which we have learned, to enable us to 'say a prayer'. That is the misuse of our Lord's famous instruction in what we call 'the Lord's Prayer'.

[1] O. Hallesby, *Prayer* (London: Inter-Varsity Fellowship, 1948), pp. 46-48.

Fourthly, prayer is not the preserve of an 'elite'—it is not an activity solely reserved for the great saints of Scripture and Christian history, or even a clerical caste. Zephaniah 3:9 speaks of a day when God will 'purify the lips of the peoples, that all of them may call on the Name of the Lord'. Even the youngest and newest believer has access to the throne of God. For this privilege, Christ's blood was shed.

Fifthly, prayer is not confined to certain 'holy places'. The Bible teaches us that wherever we are and whatever our circumstances we may 'call on the name of the Lord'. Thus Christians do not need to make pilgrimage to special places to pray. God is omnipresent in the universe, and every place can be 'holy ground'.

Where, then, can we find a definition of prayer? Well, despite the fact that it insists that prayer is the most important of all our activities (for example, *Luke* 18:1; *1 Thess.* 5:17; *Acts* 6:4), the Bible nowhere gives us a comprehensive definition of prayer. I would suggest that is because prayer defies definition. Instead, we have to ask God, as the disciples asked Jesus, 'Lord, teach us to pray'. And it will take us a lifetime to learn.

But if you insist on a definition, let me refer you to the words of John Calvin who in his commentary on Isaiah says, 'Prayer is nothing else than the opening up of our heart before God'.[1]

From the negative, I now want to turn to the positive teaching of Scripture, and ask, 'Of what does prayer consist?'. The Bible includes the following elements in true prayer:

Firstly, in prayer we are entering into God's presence through the access obtained for us in Christ's sacrificial death. So the writer of the letter to the Hebrews encourages us, 'Therefore, brothers, since we have confidence to enter the Most Holy Place by the blood of Jesus...let us draw near to God' (*Heb.* 10:19-22).

[1] John Calvin, *Commentary on the Book of the Prophet Isaiah*, Vol. 4 (Edinburgh: Calvin Translation Society, 1853), p. 353.

A second element of prayer is worshipping and adoring God for all that he is. This is the constant activity of the redeemed people of God in heaven, and we have examples of it in many parts of the book of Revelation (for example, in chapters 4 and 5). But it is also the first duty and chief delight of the believer in this world. The Psalms are full of worship and adoration, and so, for example, are the prayers of Moses, Samuel, Jeremiah, and Daniel in the Old Testament. But above all when our Lord taught the disciples to pray, as we shall find later in this book, he taught them to begin 'Our Father who art in heaven, may your name be hallowed'. That is a desire for the honour of the name or character of God, and it is to be our first concern in prayer. To see what this means, read Psalms 95 and 145, or Paul's doxology in Romans 11:33-36.

Thirdly, in prayer we are praising and thanking God for all that he does. Praise is of the essence in prayer, and yet we find that the psalmist has to call upon his soul to remember and not forget the benefits the Lord has bestowed upon him. He then recites them before God, as in Psalm 103. For the good of our own souls, we need to do the same. Talking to ourselves in this way is a sign of spiritual well-being, not of mental decay! If we develop a spirit of ingratitude and thanklessness before God, we need to remember Jesus' rebuke to the ungrateful lepers whom he had cured, and Paul's listing of ingratitude as a mark of the moral decline of the last days in 2 Timothy 3:2. The regular reading of Scripture is the best way to fuel a spirit of thankfulness.

Fourthly, prayer consists of humbling ourselves before God because of what we are, and confessing our sin and failure. This spirit is nowhere better expressed than in Ezra's prayer in Ezra 9:6: 'O my God, I am too ashamed and disgraced to lift up my face to you, my God, because our sins are higher than our heads  and our guilt has reached to the heavens'. As mere creatures before our creator, and as sinners in the presence of an infinitely holy God, we are bound to humble ourselves as we draw near to him. Confessing our sins is not just acknowledging that we are sinners. The word in the original Greek, 'homologeo', really means 'to say the same things', and the idea is that we have learned to say the same things about sin as God says, and to view it as he does. But when we confess our sins, we do not continue to brood unhealthily over our sin. Rather we glory in the fact that 'If we confess our sins, he is faithful and just and will forgive us our sins and will purify us from all unrighteousness' (*1 John* 1:9).

A fifth element of prayer is supplicating at God's throne and petitioning him for the good things for which we are totally dependent on him. What are these good things? They are the fullness of his perfect will for his children. So Jesus teaches us to pray, 'Your will be done...on earth as it is in heaven'. And the Apostle John tells us in 1 John 5:14, 'This is the confidence we have in approaching God: that if we ask anything according to his will, he hears us'. How do we know what God's will is? I know of no better answer to that question than that of John Newton, the converted slave trader. Here is an extract from a letter he wrote to a friend on the subject:

> In general, he guides and directs his people, by affording them, in answer to prayer, the light of his Holy Spirit, which enables them to understand and to love the Scriptures... By treasuring up the doctrines, precepts, promises, examples and exhortations of Scripture in their minds and daily comparing themselves with the rule by which they walk, they grow into an habitual frame of spiritual wisdom, and acquire a gracious taste, which enables them to judge of right and wrong with a degree of readiness and certainty, as a musical ear judges of sounds.[1]

---

[1] John Newton, *Letters of John Newton* (London: Banner of Truth Trust, 1960, reprint 2011), p. 88-9.

That, of course, does not mean that there is no mystery in the will of God, but it does emphasise the crying need for spiritual discernment amongst the Lord's people, which normally comes from being schooled in Scripture.

The sixth element of prayer is intercession for others. Helping his younger companion to develop a prayer ministry, Paul writes these words to Timothy in 1 Timothy 2:1: 'I urge then, first of all, that requests, prayers, intercession and thanksgiving be made for everyone'. This does not imply the kind of praying my parents heard before we went to sleep at night. I found a sure way of not being accused of leaving someone out of my prayers by saying, 'God bless everybody in the world'! Intercession involves taking the needs of a particular person or group into your heart in order to plead before God for them. It means that you have a special interest in or concern for them. You will go out of your way to learn about their needs. Someone has said, 'The network of our relationships is the sphere of our intercession'. The closer the relationship, the more intense the intercession.

Of course, the perfect example of intercession is in the ministry of our Lord Jesus Christ. He saw how vital intercession was when he warned Peter that Satan desired to sift him like wheat (*Luke* 22:31). How Peter must have trembled! 'But', said Jesus, 'I have prayed for you'. If you are a believer, you may have the same encouragement Peter must have found, because the Bible tells us that this same Jesus, now exalted at the right hand of his Father, 'ever lives to make intercession for us' (*Heb.* 7:25). An example of that intercession is in John 17, which we will consider in a later chapter. These then, in outline, are the constituent parts of biblical prayer.

## 2

# A THEOLOGICAL FOUNDATION

THE SLIGHTLY PRETENTIOUS TITLE for this chapter just means that there are a number of truths which the Bible lays before us and presses upon us in relation to prayer, and we do need to spend a little time thinking about them. They are the foundation on which we must build our thinking about prayer, and there are at the very least three of them, to which prayer is related:

a. Prayer in relation to grace
b. Prayer in relation to faith
c. Prayer in relation to Christian living

I shall say most about the first, less about the second and least about the third.

## PRAYER AND GRACE

It is very obvious in the Bible that God has made a marriage between prayer and grace, and the bond is at least threefold:

Firstly, prayer is grounded in God's grace. There is a sense in which the grand object of salvation is to bring banished sinners into the presence of God, as his reconciled children, with the cry upon their lips, 'Abba, Father'. This is what Peter is speaking about in 1 Peter 3:18, 'Christ also died for sins once for all, the righteous for the unrighteous, that he might bring us to God.' Similarly Paul tells us in Ephesians 2: 18 that the outcome of what God has done for us in Jesus' death is that 'through him we both have access to the Father'.

The ultimate problem of man in his sin is that he has no access to God, is shut out from his presence, and is not on speaking terms with him. That is why the person who is outside of Christ may try to pray but finds it is 'like speaking to someone you do not know'. Now the real problem behind that is that we cannot by ourselves do anything to put it right. We cannot gain access to God by some quality we possess by nature, or some effort we make of ourselves. The wrath of a holy God against our sin cannot be dispelled so easily. In fact, the Bible tells us that our only hope is that God may do something from his side to effect a reconciliation. It is for this reason that we shall never think rightly about prayer until we think rightly about the cross and the amazing depths to which the grace and mercy of God stooped to achieve our reconciliation to him. The great mystery to which this points is focussed in the cry of Jesus from the outer darkness of sin-bearing, 'My God, my God, why have you forsaken me?' As he travailed on the cross to bring us access to the Father, Jesus was himself denied that access and experienced the reality of that dereliction which is really the inaccessibility of God. But what he is doing in this astonishing display of God's grace, his undeserved love to sinners, is enabling them to 'enter the holiest by the blood of Jesus'.

Prayer is therefore grounded on God's saving grace in Jesus Christ, and the sheer wonder of what this meant made it impossible for the apostles to think lightly of the privilege of access to the Father.

Secondly, prayer is also an evidence of grace. As the evidence of life is a cry, so the evidence of grace and sonship is the cry 'Abba, Father'. Thus it is that Paul's experience of God's grace on the Damascus road was ratified to Ananias in Acts 9:11 by the Lord pointing to a simple fact: 'Behold he is praying'. Of course, as a devout Pharisee, Paul had said prayers diligently and frequently in the past. But he was now discovering the difference between saying prayers and praying. Jesus himself illustrates this distinction in his picture of the proud Pharisee in the temple, who having no awareness of needing to deal with God on the basis of free grace, 'prays with himself' (*Luke* 18:11) whereas the publican could not bring himself to lift up his head, but beat his breast and cried to God for mercy. In Acts 9:11, Paul is in the place of the publican, and this humbling of his proud Pharisaic spirit is a true evidence of grace. Indeed the Bible tells us that it is possible to recognise the true child of God because he 'calls on the Father' (*1 Pet.* 1:17), which is the ultimate contrast with the ungodly who 'do not call on the Lord' (*Psa.* 14:4). Prayer is thus an evidence of grace.

Thirdly, prayer is a means of grace. God is not only sovereign and gracious; he also delights to be entreated by his children, and has decreed certain means by which his grace is brought to us. Prayer is one of these. This is the truth which lies behind so much of Jesus' teaching on prayer, as we shall discover a little later. He teaches us to ask, seek and knock, that the riches of the Father's grace may become ours.

Paul likewise sets an example to the churches of how central a praying ministry is in seeking the spiritual growth of a church. He frequently tells his correspondents how constantly he prays for them (for example, in *Col.* 1:9) and recognises that the Colossians' growth in grace and in the knowledge of God and their fruitfulness in life and service would primarily be furthered by his praying for them. He was praying them *on* spiritually. He also recognised that the fruitfulness and effectiveness of his ministry was closely linked to the faithful praying of the churches. Only God knows how much we need such truth to dawn upon the church and her ministers in our own time.

Prayer is a means of God's grace. If we really believed that, and took it seriously, then prayer would become fundamental, instead of supplemental, in all our thinking about Christian work and service.

## PRAYER AND FAITH

Prayer is linked with faith in Scripture in the sense described in Hebrews 11:6: 'Whoever would draw near to God must believe that he exists, and that he rewards those who seek him.' In other words, it is our understanding of God, in his nature and character, that most deeply affects our praying. It is the characteristic of faith to focus not upon itself but upon its object. The prayer of faith is therefore prayer which rests upon the glorious character of God, which is why Hudson Taylor, founder of the China Inland Mission, said so often, 'It is not great faith we need so much as faith in a great God.' In prayer faith reaches out to three particular aspects of God's being.

First to his *character as the Sovereign Lord of the universe*. So we speak of coming to 'the throne of grace' and acknowledge that God rules over all that he has made. The apostles remind God of this in the prayer we find in Acts 4:24-30: 'Sovereign Lord', they cry, 'you made the heaven and the earth and the sea and everything in them.' The same appeal to God's character is made in Abraham's prayer in Genesis 18, in Jehoshaphat's in 2 Chronicles 20, and in Jeremiah's in Jeremiah 32.

Secondly, in prayer faith reaches out to *God's promises*, and trusts that every word he has spoken will come to pass. So Christians often speak about 'pleading the promises of God' and asking him to fulfil what he has said in his word. For example, when the believer falls into sin, he or she must immediately plead God's promise in 1 John 1:9 about his willingness when we confess our sin to cleanse us from it, and pray that we may receive what God has promised.

Thirdly, in prayer faith reaches out to *the good and perfect will of God*. The great scriptural example of this is our Lord Jesus Christ in Gethsemane, recorded for us in Matthew 26:39. There Jesus is facing the awful prospect of bearing our sin and God's wrath on Calvary, but what he beseeches the Father for is 'not my will but your will'. Here is one of the most vital lessons we could ever learn about prayer. The prayer of faith is not a petulant insistence on getting what we want, but a trustful confidence in the Father's wisdom, love and care for his own.

In the light of this, it will be seen how vital is the relation between our attitude to Scripture and our prayer life. It is the Christian whose heart and mind are filled with the knowledge of God's will and ways and character who will pray the prayer of faith. 'Faith', writes John Calvin, 'rests not on ignorance, but on knowledge'". So it is that in that long psalm (*Psa.* 119), petition after petition is made 'according to your word'.

## PRAYER AND CHRISTIAN LIVING

It is impossible to separate someone's prayer life from the rest of their life as a Christian. That is why in Matthew's Gospel, the Lord's Prayer is embedded within the Sermon on the Mount, the purpose of which is to teach the disciples how to live. The Lord's Prayer is indeed a pattern prayer, as is often said. But before it is a pattern for praying, it must be a pattern for living, and for this reason: no man or woman can make the priorities of the Lord's Prayer the language of their own prayers, unless they are also the priorities of one's own life. The very thing Jesus warns against, in the context of Matthew 6, is a divorce between the heart and the lips, resulting in the hypocrisy which intends prayer for the ears of men rather than the ears of God. This is the root of praying in

[1] John Calvin, *Institutes of the Christian Religion*, trans. F. L. Battles, ed. J. T. McNeill (Philadelphia: Westminster Press, 1960), III. II. 2.

public for things we don't really want, but since we think it would be spiritual to want them if we did, we say we do! No divorce is more tragic than this one.

We therefore need to ask ourselves, 'Do I really want the hallowing of God's name, the extension of his kingdom and the rule of his will more than all else in my life—even more than my daily bread? Are these really the priorities by which I live?'. So it is that in prayer as well as everywhere else, the person I am is of infinitely greater significance than the words I speak.

Now, lest we be daunted or discouraged, let us take encouragement from the gracious provision God has made for his children as they pray. He has taught us that the entire Godhead conspires together to aid us. The Father assures us from his throne of his sovereign power ('There is nothing too hard for you'—*Jer.* 32:17). The Son is ascended to the Father's right hand, ever living to make intercession for us (*Rom.* 8:34). And the blessed Holy Spirit indwells every child of the Father, and when we find in our weakness that we do not know what to pray for as we ought, 'He intercedes for us with sighs too deep for words' (*Rom.* 8:26).

So when we ask of God, 'Lord teach us to pray', it is true that there is nothing he would rather do. But it may cost us more than we first thought.

# 3

# THE TEACHING OF JESUS
# ON PRAYER (1)

W HEN ONE IS PLANNING A BOOK on the subject of prayer, it would be entirely commendable to turn to the lives of the great men and women of God through the ages and draw upon what they teach us. We could all think of a long line of such people. The fact that I shall not be appealing to them is not a sign that I am less than grateful for the rich teaching and example they have left us. Rather, it is that they are all imperfect, fallen people like ourselves. It is incomparably safer to put ourselves under the instruction of the Lord Jesus Christ himself who has left us a substantial body of teaching about prayer and a perfect example of praying recorded in the Gospels. We should remind ourselves that he is the one who has been in a perfect relationship with his Father through all eternity, and while experiencing all our infirmities during his ministry on earth, nonetheless was in perfect communion with the Father throughout these years. He alone is our perfect teacher, and our perfect example.

There are a number of occasions in the Gospels where Jesus teaches his disciples about prayer. None is better known than the classic occasion in Matthew chapter 6 when he teaches them what we call the 'Lord's Prayer'.

Introducing ourselves to the content of this prayer, there are three things we need to notice briefly:

# PRAYER, A BIBLICAL PERSPECTIVE

a) Although we call this prayer in Matthew 6 the 'Lord's Prayer', it is not a prayer that Jesus ever prayed, or indeed could pray. The reason is simply that it contains a prayer for forgiveness in verse 12, and the Lord Jesus Christ was without sin, as Paul reminds us in 2 Corinthians 5:21. He therefore could never pray these words.

b) The prayer is not intended to be repeated *verbatim* by us. It is rather a pattern for prayer, to teach us to pray ourselves. The warning against relying on words alone in verse 7 would teach us the danger of empty repetition. That is not to say that we should never repeat the Lord's Prayer. It would be our loss not to do so, but it would be a greater loss to treat this prayer as a kind of talisman, the repetition of which would bring us some special blessing.

c) The location of this prayer in the middle of the Sermon on the Mount in Matthew chapters 5-7 has much significance. The sermon is Jesus' teaching about living our lives as members of his kingdom, and children of the Father. That means that I cannot detach my 'prayer life' from the rest of my life as a Christian. We pray as we live, and we live as we pray. Let me give you a very obvious example of this. You cannot pray 'Your will be done', unless the will of God is the supreme issue in your life, which you desire above everything else. So we do not learn to pray in isolation from learning to live a God-honouring and God-glorifying life.

In his teaching on prayer in Matthew 6:5-15, Jesus deals with two main subjects: firstly, the manner in which we should pray; and secondly, the matters about which we should pray. We shall approach these subjects in that way.

Firstly, we should consider the manner in which we should pray. There are three things to which Jesus draws our attention in verses 5, 6 and 7, and they are each introduced with the words 'when you pray'. The subject in verse 5 is sincerity; in verse 6 it is secrecy; while in verse 7 it is simplicity.

## SINCERITY (verse 5)

Now, hypocrisy is a horrible thing in any sphere of life. But it is never more ugly than in the place of prayer, where we may pray to impress other people, rather than to be heard by God. Jesus' warning in verse 5 is that if the hypocrite puts on his act to please men, he will receive his reward from them. But he will receive nothing from God.

## SECRECY (verse 6)

When Jesus says, 'When you pray, go into your room, close the door and pray to your Father who is unseen. Then your Father who sees what is done in secret will reward you', he is not saying, 'Never pray with others' (for example, in a prayer meeting). If you think of it, that could hardly be so, since he teaches the disciples to pray '*Our* Father'. What Jesus is saying is that however else we may pray, we must shut out every other consideration except the presence of the Father. Private, secret prayer is the essential background to public, communal prayer. Someone once wrote in his journal, 'Only the reality of "praying in secret" could safeguard the sincerity of praying in public'.

## SIMPLICITY (verses 7-8)

Here Jesus is referring to pagans praying to pagan gods. And in pagan religion, one of the principles was that much repetition and many words were a persuasive means of getting the gods to hear and answer. The same can be illustrated from pagan religion today. Jesus says, 'Do not be like them'. Again, we need to be clear that Jesus is not here forbidding repetition in prayer. He himself repeated the same words three times in prayer in Gethsemane. What he is warning against is a mindless, heartless piling up of mere words. He is pleading for a simple expression of true desire.

That then is the manner in which Jesus teaches us to pray.

But secondly, we come to consider the matters about which we should pray. I often think that the primary truth Jesus is teaching us here are the priorities which should occupy us when we pray. Have you noticed that the first half of the prayer is entirely taken up with God—his nature, his name, his kingdom or rule, and his will or pleasure? There is not a mention of any request until we are half way through the prayer at verse 11.

Now, that emphasis from Jesus' teaching turns much common thinking about prayer on its head, does it not? When people say, 'Do you believe in prayer?', they almost always mean 'Do you believe prayer is an effective means for obtaining some benefit you need?'. But Jesus tells us that the heart of the true disciple is set on the glory and the purposes of God, our Father in heaven. Notice the significance of the ways in which Jesus refers to God:

a) *Our Father*. The word Father is used in two ways in the New Testament: In one instance, it is used inclusively of all men and women—for example, by Paul in Athens in Acts 17:27-29. He refers to God as our creator and goes on to say, 'We are his offspring'. But that is a minority use and only refers to our creatureliness. The majority use is of God as the one who becomes our Father when we are born from above through the Holy Spirit. It is the Holy Spirit alone who enables us to cry 'Abba, Father' (*Rom.* 8:15). Of course, anyone may call God 'Father', but apart from the work of the Holy Spirit within us, it is a meaningless title.

b) *in Heaven*. There are three ways in which the Bible uses this phrase: the first is of 'the sky above us' (an example would be 'the birds of heaven'). The second is of the heavens beyond us, that is, the firmament in which are the sun, moon and stars. The third is the one used here by Jesus. It is the sphere in which God lives and reigns, without any boundaries or limitations. So God is our Father, but he is not like an earthly father—he has no limitations of any kind, and that is vital for us to recognise as we pray.

Now notice what things we are to pray for with regard to God: Firstly, we are to pray for the hallowing of God's name. The name of God in Scripture is of course another way of speaking of his character or nature. To hallow God's name means not 'to make his name holy' but to reverence, or glorify, or honour his great name. God's name is already holy and we cannot add to that, but we long that the holiness which caused the angels to veil their faces in Isaiah 6 might dawn upon our contemporaries and upon ourselves. Another way of saying all this is to say that we begin our praying with worship, not with our wants.

Secondly, we are to pray for the coming of God's kingdom. God's kingdom is simply the sphere in which he rules as king. When we pray, 'Your kingdom come', we are expressing the desire that God's reign may be extended both in the lives of his people (that he may be Lord of more and more of our life) and in the world he has made. There will, we are assured in Philippians 2:9-11, come a day when 'every knee shall bow, and every tongue confess that Jesus Christ is Lord, to the glory of God the Father'. We are praying in this part of the Lord's Prayer, for the coming of that day and the consummation of God's kingdom.

Thirdly, we are to pray for the doing of God's will. Jesus here teaches us to pray for heaven on earth! The point is that there is only one place where the will of God is done perfectly, and that is in heaven. There the saints of God in glory experience perfect joy. The lives of his people in this world will reach their truest fulfilment nowhere else but in the very centre of the will of God. Praying 'May your will be done on earth as it is in heaven' is, of course, a missionary prayer. Notice that the advance of the kingdom through the preaching of the gospel takes precedence in this prayer over our own physical needs—to which Jesus now turns.

Fourthly, therefore, we are to pray for our physical, material needs. 'Give us this day our daily bread' is a prayer for the supply of all our physical needs. For both our physical and spiritual needs, Jesus is reminding us that we are totally dependent on God. Since our physical needs are more apparent to us than anything else, he begins here, but there is no need, physical, emotional, spiritual, intellectual or psychological for which we are not utterly, personally and daily dependent on our heavenly Father. Giving thanks for our food before we eat at every meal is a token and expression of that dependence, both for the poorest of us economically, and for the most affluent.

Fifthly, we are to pray for our spiritual needs. 'Forgive us our debts as we forgive our debtors', is a prayer that reminds us of our deep-seated need not only for God's grace in providing our material needs but for his rich mercy in the cleansing of our conscience from the defilement of sin. Of course the world does not see that need, nor specially care about it, and we may even try to ignore it. But it will not go away, and even if it matters less than it used to for us, it matters deeply to God. Just as we need daily bread, so we need daily forgiveness. We cannot have true communion with God apart from this. And we will not know the joy of forgiveness for ourselves if we have not extended it to others, so Jesus adds 'as we also have forgiven our debtors ... for if you forgive men when they sin against you, your heavenly Father will also forgive you. But if you do not forgive men their sins, your Father will not forgive your sins'. These two are bound together by God. We are not forgiven because we forgive others, but we cannot receive forgiveness without forgiving others.

And sixthly, we are to pray for our continuing need of divine protection: verse 13 reads, 'And lead us not into temptation, but deliver us from the evil one'. The first part of that petition may arrest our attention. Would God lead us into temptation? Well, the short answer to that is that the Holy Spirit drove our Lord into the wilderness to be tempted by the devil (*Matt.* 4:1). That

agonising experience was part of the Father's perfect work of re-
demption for our sake. Behind this petition, there lies the awareness of our own weakness and liability to fall before the fierce on-
slaught of the devil. So we pray that the Father may spare us the
worst testing. You see, there are two features associated with every
temptation. There is the desire on the one hand, and the opportunity on the other. Sometimes we may have the desire, but the opportunity is removed. At other times we may have the opportunity,
but the desire is removed. When desire and opportunity coincide,
we are really in the fires of temptation. It is then that we need to
be reminded of the promise of 1 Corinthians 10:13: 'God is faithful;
he will not let you be tempted beyond what you can bear', and pray
'Father, deliver!'

Indeed, his is the kingdom, and the power and the glory
forever.

# 4

# THE TEACHING OF JESUS
# ON PRAYER (2)

*Ask and it will be given to you; seek and you will find; knock and the
door will be opened to you. For everyone who asks receives; he who
seeks finds; and to him who knocks, the door will be opened. Which of
you, if his son asks for bread, will give him a stone? Or if he asks for
a fish, will give him a snake? If you, then, though you are evil, know
how to give good gifts to your children, how much more will your
Father in heaven give good gifts to those who ask him! So in everything, do to others what you would have them do to you, for this
sums up the Law and the Prophets.*

MATTHEW 7:7-12

THIS SHORT PASSAGE IN MATTHEW 7 is still part of the
Sermon on the Mount. Like so many parts of the Bible, it
is trinitarian in its form: there are three parts to it.  That
may be why so many sermons have three points!

In verse 7, Jesus presents us with three precepts or commands:
'ask, seek and knock'. In verse 8 he sets before us a threefold series of
promises to encourage us: 'For everyone who asks receives; he who
seeks finds; and to him who knocks, the door will be opened'. Finally
in verses 9-11, Jesus uses the form of a parable to demonstrate how
willing God is to give good gifts to those who ask him.

## *THE PRECEPTS* (verse 7)

Many students of the Sermon on the Mount have wondered whether we are intended to see a distinction between these three precepts—ask, seek, knock—or whether we should think of them as just a repetition of the same idea. Personally, I do not think they are a mere repetition. More likely they seem to be an *intensification* with a different focus, and that is how we shall approach them here.

It is obvious that grammatically all three of them are present imperatives—they are commands which imply, 'go on continuing to do this'. That is, these are not exhortations for special occasions—perhaps when we are in exceptionally difficult circumstances or some unusual crisis. Rather, this is a way of life. We are, whether we realise it or not, in constant dependence upon God, and we should therefore constantly appeal to him and persevere in doing so.

Let me put these three precepts to you in this way: Firstly, be a *suppliant*: 'Ask'. Let me press upon you the biblical necessity of asking. If, as we learn from Jesus in Matthew 6:8, our Father knows the things we need before we ask him, why should it be so important that we ask? Or to put it another way, 'Why is prayer necessary?' It is certainly not to inform God about something he did not already know! Let us approach the answer this way:

Primarily, this is a command of God. We therefore ask because he tells us to do so. James 4:2 tells us, 'You do not have, because you do not ask God'. But there is more.

It appears from Scripture that God not only commands us to ask, but that part of his perfect and glorious character is that he delights to be entreated by his children—even by his only begotten Son. For this truth, we need to go to Psalm 2, which is a messianic psalm. In verses 7 to 8, God is speaking to his Son and says, 'You are my Son, today I have become your Father. Ask of me, and I will make the nations your inheritance, the ends of the earth your possession'. You may know that that psalm is quoted in Revelation 2:27, and is there applied by Christ to himself. The point is that the Father delights to give when his children ask. So supplication has a special place in God the Father's purposes.

Secondly, be a *seeker*: 'Seek and you will find'. Now again, I am not entirely sure that we can fathom the reason for this, but there is no doubt whatsoever that Scripture teaches us that God responds to those who seek him. We need to listen to the repeated emphasis on this in the Bible:

Jeremiah 29:13: 'You will seek me and you will find me when you seek me with all your heart'.

2 Chronicles 7:14: 'If my people who are called by my name will humble themselves and pray, and seek my face…, then will I hear from heaven…'

Isaiah 55:6: 'Seek the Lord while he may be found, call upon him while he is near'.

Psalm 119:10: 'With my whole heart I have sought you'.

Proverbs 8:17: 'They that seek me find me'.

There is little doubt in my own mind that this is not a repetition of the earlier command 'ask', but rather an intensification. Notice the focus of our seeking: it is God—not things from him, but God himself that we seek. Seeking also involves perseverance and the commitment of time, whereas asking does not.

Thirdly, be *serious*: 'Knock and the door will be opened to you'. Again, I think this is an intensification of seeking. It is of great significance that in Luke's Gospel, the Lord's Prayer is followed immediately by the parable known as 'the parable of the importunate friend'. It is the story of someone who has a friend to whom he goes at midnight to ask for bread to feed a visitor who, in the course of a journey, arrives at his house. The host has been 'caught out' with no food, hence the late night request. The friend is naturally reluctant to be disturbed, but Jesus says that it is the persistence and perseverance of the request and the seriousness of the man asking which makes him ready to rise and respond. When I lived in Ayrshire in Scotland, they used to tell of the laziest man anyone had met. He was a meter reader with the Gas Board, but wanted to avoid the trouble of going into the home, finding the meter and using his torch to read the figures and then write them in his book. So when he knocked on the door he would do so with such gentleness that scarcely anyone would hear. Now when we knock on a door, it is *access* we are seeking. But this man was not serious about gaining access. He lost his job, of course, because he was not serious. God responds to seriousness. Dilettantes and spiritual playboys are unlikely to engage his heart and mind. Do you know what it is like if someone does not treat you seriously? It is not just disappointing. It is demeaning.

So Jesus presses upon us these three things: Be a supplicant, be a seeker, and be serious. True prayer demands all three.

## *THE PROMISES* (verse 8)

Note that the point of verse 8 is to reinforce the commands Jesus gives us with promises to those who obey them. They are in the indicative mood, stating facts: those who ask actually receive; those who seek do indeed find, and the one who knocks does gain entry. John Calvin says, 'Nothing is adapted better to excite us to prayer than a full conviction that we shall be heard.' But we find it difficult to apply these promises to our own prayer life, because we are weak and sinful and inconsequential. Our tendency is to think this applies to the great praying giants, but Jesus is saying that this is true for every child of God. The throne of God to which we come is

'John Calvin, *Commentary on a Harmony of the Evangelists: Matthew, Mark and Luke*, Vol. I (Edinburgh: Calvin Translation Society, 1845), p. 351.

a throne of grace, and no believer is ever insignificant there. The only argument we need is that the occupant of the throne is our Father.

So these are the precepts and promises Jesus provides for us as we pray. But finally in this passage there is the parable in which Jesus emphasises his teaching.

## THE PARABLE (verses 9-11)

This parable is of course built on the argument which is familiar in the Bible—the argument from the lesser to the greater or the 'how much more' argument, as it is often called. The comparison here is between the actions of an imperfect human father and the acts of a divine and perfect heavenly father. Jesus challenges his listeners: 'Which of you, if his son asks for bread, will give him a stone? Or if he asks for a fish, will give him a snake?' The very idea would be incomprehensible in relation to our own fathers, and yet Jesus says in verse 11, 'You are evil'. That is, our character is corrupted by sin. And yet we can be relied upon not to act in that corrupt way towards our own children! Now, how infinitely more can we rely on the perfect, untarnished and incorruptible character of our heavenly Father to do nothing but good for his children?

You will notice the other way this argument develops. It employs the elementary teaching method of moving from the familiar to the unfamiliar. The familiar is the world of earthly fatherhood, with so much in it that is good, and yet it is imperfect and tainted by sin. The unfamiliar is the world of the perfect fatherhood of God, who never makes mistakes, never lacks perfect wisdom and knowledge and always gives to his children only what is good for them. Now the lesson is that we ought unhesitatingly to put our trust in our Father in heaven when we pray, and believe that his answer will be as perfect as his character. Therefore we can ask, seek and knock with the utmost confidence.

# 5

# THE EXAMPLE OF JESUS
## IN JOHN 17

I N THE LAST TWO CHAPTERS, we have considered two places in Matthew's Gospel where Jesus sets out his teaching on prayer for his disciples. It may be true for most of us that even more effective than someone's teaching, is their example of how they do what they are instructing us to do. So we often ask, 'Show us how to do it'. Do you think this is one reason why Jesus allows the disciples to overhear him pray? I think myself that it may be.

This prayer of our Lord recorded in John 17 is certainly one of the most sublime and remarkable utterances in the whole of literature. Since the sixteenth century, it has been called 'the high priestly prayer of our Lord'. That description points us to the fact that Jesus is here the only mediator between God and men, appearing before the Father on behalf of his own, with his mind and spirit occupied with his coming death. That latter truth is illustrated by the very first words Jesus utters—'Father the hour has come'. The phrase is charged with meaning. Since the second chapter of John, Jesus has spoken about 'his hour' ('my hour has not yet come' in John 2:4). That phrase is repeated many times in the Gospel, and 'the hour' always refers to the hour of his death for sin. Not until this point does Jesus say 'the hour has come', that is, he has arrived at that moment for which he came into the world, the moment when on the cross he will be lifted up and will glorify the Father.

Now to 'glorify the Father' is to reveal the Father's true character and the real wonder of his being. How can the cross do that? Well if you think of it, where else in the universe is the goodness and mercy and love and righteousness of God displayed as in the sacrificial death of Jesus? John Calvin beautifully says, 'In the Cross of Christ, as in a magnificent theatre, the inestimable goodness of God is displayed before the whole world'.[1] So Jesus opens his heart to the Father. There are three great emphases in his prayer:

Firstly, *Jesus is absorbed with the glory of the Godhead* in verses 1-5. 'Glorify your Son, that your Son may glorify you' (verse 1). Notice that this is not a selfish prayer for his own glory which comes from the Saviour's lips. He is truly absorbed with the glory of the Godhead, and from verse 2 through to verse 5 he reflects upon the purpose of the Father, stretching from eternity past in verse 2 to eternity future in verse 5, from the authority the Father gave him before the foundation of the world in verse 2 (compare with Psalm 2) to the resumption of his glory in verse 5. That glory is a glory shared with the Father, whose glory has been the passion of the Lord Jesus Christ's life and ministry as he declares in verse 4. He sums up his ministry, completing the work the Father gave him to do, in the words, 'I have brought you glory on earth'.

Now this example of our Lord needs to be written on the hearts of his disciples. They too must be absorbed with the glory of the Godhead, and reflect the great priority in our Lord's prayer: a passion for the glory of God. There is no other acceptable ultimate motive in prayer than this. Can you think of what it would mean to come to the last hours of your life and be able to say 'I have brought you glory on earth'?

Secondly, *Jesus is burdened by the needs of his own* in verses 6-19. It is unmistakeably clear in this passage that the needs of his own

[1]John Calvin, *Commentary on the Gospel of John*, Vol. 2 (Edinburgh: Calvin Translation Society, 1847), p. 73.

lie closest to the heart of Jesus. Keep reminding yourself of that precious truth. It is true for several reasons:

a) Because they are the Father's gift to the Lord Jesus. Look at the last section of verse 2, 'all those you have given to him', and at verse 6, 'I have revealed you to those you gave me out of the world', and at verse 9, 'I pray for them . . . for those you have given me'. Do you see what this means? This is how Christ comes to have a people. This is how you came to be Christ's: you were given to him by the Father. This is how Christ the bridegroom gains his bride, the church. They are given to him by the Father. Have you been at a wedding when the clergyman has a man and a woman before him? He asks, 'Who gives this woman to be married to this man?' and the bride's father says, 'I do', and he makes the greatest gift he ever gives—he hands the bride over to the bridegroom. That is actually a picture of what happens when the sinner comes to Christ. The question is, 'Who gives this sinner to be united to the only Saviour?' And God the Father answers, 'I do'. So Jesus says, 'You gave them to me'.

b) Because they are the instruments of his glory. In the last section of verse 10 we have, 'Glory has come to me through them'. Someone has said that this is the most generous thing Jesus ever said about his disciples. Of course he is making a statement of faith: this is certainly the destiny of his disciples and his purpose for them, and though they deny him and disown him, yet he will have glory through them in the end.

c) Because they are left in a hostile world (verses 11-14). 'Holy Father, protect them by the power of your name'. These words must have been an immeasurable comfort to these weak disciples. Notice the things Jesus asks the Father for them: three times—in verses 11, 12 and 15—he prays for their protection. He recognises how vulnerable they are in the world. He has protected them while he was in the world and now he confidently commits them to the

Father's care. The second thing he prays for is unity (end of verse 11 and verses 21-23), 'that all of them may be one'. Jesus was aware that the unity they knew in the upper room at Pentecost would be fragile. The evil one (verse 15) would do everything in his power to fracture that unity and set them against each other. He also prayed for holiness (verse 17)—their greatest need would be that the world might see the image of the glory of God in them (verse 22).

The world in which Jesus leaves them is described in his prayer in three ways: it is a *foreign field* (verse 14)—'the world has hated them, for they are not of the world any more than I am of the world'. So we must not be surprised if we experience something of the 'homelessness of the human spirit' in this godless world. It is a *battlefield* (verse 15) because the evil one is on the warpath in the world, and we are therefore engaged, as Paul warns us, in a warfare which at times will be fierce (*Eph.* 6:11-12). It is a *mission field* (verse 18)—'As you sent me into the world, I have sent them into the world'. We are therefore neither to flee out of the world, nor to conform to the world, but to be missionaries in the world, sent by the Saviour himself.

But the vital truth is that just as the Lord Jesus Christ intercedes with the Father for the security, unity, holiness and usefulness of the first disciples, so he lives at the right hand of God, making intercession for us—'Father keep him, keep her, now in this hour of need'. Listen to the biblical warrant for this belief in Hebrews 7:25: 'Therefore he is able to save completely those who come to God through him, because he always lives to intercede for them'.

Finally, verses 20 to 26 of John 17 tell us that *Jesus is distressed because the world does not know God.* The New International Version does less than justice to verse 25, where Jesus cries out, 'O righteous Father, the world does not know you'. This is the ultimate tragedy of the world and of worldly men and women: they do not know God. No other element in their plight is as serious as this; neither economic nor physical need compares to it. And this ought to be the ultimate distress in our hearts as we pray for the world around us and beyond us. Notice that Jesus has a concern not only for his own generation but for generations to come—'I pray also for those who will believe in me through their message' (verse 20). We should share our Lord's burden for the future church, perhaps especially for children within our own family circle, and for those as yet unborn.

These verses reveal to us the deep concern Jesus has for both unity in the church, and evangelism in the world. In the mind of Jesus the two are connected: 'May they be brought to complete unity, to let the world know that you sent me'. Unfortunately, recent emphasis has focussed on institutional unity in the church, whereas Jesus is primarily referring to spiritual unity (as in verse 22, 'that they may be one as we are one'). Biblical unity is not something that can be achieved by organisation. It is organic rather than organisational, the product of the Holy Spirit's work rather than that of conferences and committees. Of course you can produce union and unification by human means, but not unity. A perceptive preacher once said, 'If you tie two cats' tails together you will have union, but certainly not unity!' Nor does unity imply uniformity. But true Christian unity does imply unanimity about gospel truth—that is, we need to be of one mind regarding the message we preach. Nothing beclouds the mind of the unbeliever more than one professing Christian preacher contradicting the message of another.

It is however true that we are committed here by Jesus to strive for unity in the church of God. Do you ever pray for unity in your own church? Do you ever ask yourself, 'Am I a peacemaker or a peacebreaker in my church?'. It was Thomas Manton, the seventeenth century Puritan, who piercingly said, 'Division in the church leads to atheism in the world'.

## PRAYER, A BIBLICAL PERSPECTIVE

Before leaving this remarkable intercessory prayer of our Lord, we do need to allow his example to challenge us about our own intercessions, not only at times of special need, but perseveringly for those not yet brought to a knowledge of Christ, those who are young in the faith, who need to be 'prayed on', and those who are not naturally amongst our 'friends'. We do need to ask God also for a vision for the next generation, that we might have a sense of history and destiny about our intercessions. My mother had an elderly aunt who died long before I was born. She lived in my grandparents' home and used to pray aloud in her room every night. My mother and her sister and brothers used to listen to her 'talking to herself' as they thought, and asking for God's hand to be upon her sister (my grandmother), and 'her children and her children's children'. They used to chant in playful mockery outside her door. But when my mother told us about this, my brother said to me, 'Isn't that amazing? She was praying for us long before we were born'. We often wonder what part that old lady had in the invasion of grace into our family. Lord, teach us to pray!

# 6

# THE PRIORITY OF THE APOSTLES

*Brothers, choose seven men from among you who are known to
be full of the Spirit and wisdom. We will turn this responsibility
over to them and will give our attention to prayer and
the ministry of the word.*

ACTS 6:3-4

I T WOULD BE DIFFICULT to exaggerate the importance of this
brief passage in Acts 6. Someone has described it as 'The first
definitive reformation in the Apostolic Church.' Its relevance
for us is quite simple. It is that amongst our greatest needs in the
contemporary church is a similar reformation, and a comparable
re-assessment of our priorities.

The establishing of priorities is always a vital issue, simply because
we all suffer from limitations, whether of energy, time, money or other
resources. That is true of large organisations as well as individuals.
No one has infinite resources, except God. To fail to establish clear
priorities means that we become the servant of whatever pressure
group is strongest or most persuasive. In this situation, the apostles
were not only motivated by available resources but by the essential
factor of *calling*. They had to ask, 'What has God particularly *called*
us to do?' It was the answer to that question which produced the
settlement described in this chapter.

You may be familiar with the apparently trivial circumstances
which precipitated what happened. In the context of the growth

PRAYER, A BIBLICAL PERSPECTIVE

of the church, there developed an important ministry to the social needs of the widows in the church. There was an ethnic distinction between the Hellenistic and Hebraic widows. The former felt they were being neglected, and a divisive spirit of murmuring began in the church. Now the apostles regarded this as sufficiently important for them to call a kind of 'general assembly' (verse 2) to deal with the issue. The peril they saw was that of neglecting the God-given priorities associated with their calling in order to keep everybody happy. Their verdict on that possibility was, 'It would not be right' for them to neglect the things that were God-ordained priorities in order to deal with other vital matters, however important. They then made alternative but satisfactory and sensible arrangements, described in verse 3, and you will find their resolve for themselves in verse 4: 'We will devote ourselves to prayer and the ministry of the word.' Now that decision not only pleased the people (verse 5). It more importantly pleased God, who gave prosperity to the progress of the Word of God and multiplied the number of disciples in Jerusalem (verse 7). The conclusion we must draw is that if we are going to be apostolic in the pattern of our church life, we need to adopt the same priorities.

This is not to suggest for a moment that a concern for the material and physical needs of the poor and deprived was unimportant. The fact that the apostles went to such lengths to meet the material needs of these widows is evidence of how deep was their care: as also was the calibre of people the church chose to undertake the task (for example, Stephen was 'a man full of faith and of the Holy Spirit'—verse 8). But above all, there was something else of supreme importance, and that was 'prayer and the ministry of the word'. To these, the apostolic band determined to give themselves without reservation or distraction. It is my deepest conviction that God is calling his church in the twenty-first century to re-echo this holy determination of the first century apostles. We must now turn to examine these priorities more closely, particularly, in the context of this book, the priority of prayer.

## THE PRIORITY OF PRAYER (verse 4)

'We will give ourselves continually to prayer' (AV)

'We will give our attention to prayer' (NIV)

'We will devote ourselves to prayer' (ESV)

'We will continue steadfastly in prayer' (ASV)

This verse, given in different versions above, is not simply saying that prayer is important and that every Christian should pray and every church should have a prayer meeting. What it is saying is that one of the primary functions of the church is prayer, and the greatest need of a needy world is a praying church, and the greatest need of a moribund church is praying leaders. Let me spell this out a little more in two *propositions* which arise from the context of this passage in Acts:

Firstly, prayer is the basic form of Christian service. Of course we are *not* saying prayer is the only form of Christian service, but that it is the basic one. Look at the language they use: 'We will reserve our best energies—our very bodily resources—for prayer'. It was not that they were avoiding the hardest work in the church. They were actually *choosing* it, because it is a consistent theme in Scripture that prayer *is work*. Paul cries out in Romans 15:30: 'Strive together with me in your prayers to God for me', and he uses the word which really means 'to agonise'.

In the Christian church over the years, we have turned the truth upside down, and commonly speak of 'praying for the work'—the implication being that prayer is an additional ingredient to our Christian service. The truth is that prayer *is* the real work, and apart from it all other work is in vain. The reason for that is quite simple. It is that essentially this work in which we are engaged is God's work, not man's. There are endless lists of things that men and women can do: we can intellectually convince people, we can emotionally move them and we can materially improve them. But only God can spiritually resurrect them out of spiritual death into life in Christ; only God can convict their conscience and convince them of their need of a Saviour; only God can open the eyes of the spiritually blind and give them sight; and only God can transform their character and recreate them into the image of Christ. And, my dear friends who read this book, *that is the essence of the work in which we are engaged.* So Paul tells us in 1 Corinthians 3:6, 'I planted the seed, Apollos watered it, but God made it grow. So neither he who plants nor he who waters is anything, but only God who makes things grow.' Now if the conversion of sinners is God's work, the simple question we must ask and answer is, 'To whom do we apply to have this work done?' The only answer logically as well as theologically is 'to God'. That is why prayer is fundamental rather than supplemental in all our service. That is why the primary evangelistic method is prayer.

Secondly, prayer is the basic form of Christian warfare. It was clearly Christian warfare in which the apostolic church was engaged. There is a discernible pattern in the Book of Acts of every advance of the gospel being met with a counter-thrust from the kingdom of darkness. This is apparent as early as chapter 4 when Peter and John are brought before the Sanhedrin, in the aftermath of the blessing associated with the healing of the crippled beggar and the powerful preaching of Peter. The result of that meeting was that they were silenced (*Acts* 4:18). Then the church went to prayer (*Acts* 4:24ff). The next phase was one of great blessing in the church, including an outpouring of generosity in giving (*Acts* 4:32-37). However, that was followed by the episode of Ananias and Sapphira who lied to the apostles—their hearts, according to the apostles, filled by Satan (*Acts* 5:3). Their hypocrisy brought the judgment of God upon them. Thereafter God was pleased to bless a church which had been cleansed and many were added to their number (*Acts* 5:14). Subsequently, the Sanhedrin again arrested them but a Pharisee named Gamaliel spoke in their favour and they were flogged and released, and 'never stopped teaching and proclaiming the good news that Jesus is the Christ' (*Acts* 5:42). It was at this point that the attack from the devil came from inside the church at the beginning of chapter 6. Division and murmuring, as we have seen, broke out.

This warfare is the normal pattern for the church of Jesus Christ, but there is a vital question for those who are involved in it. It is, 'Where is the front line in this warfare?' Anyone who knows anything about waging a war knows that this is the primary question. I had an uncle who was in the First World War. He used to regale us with stories about his exploits. I am sure they lost nothing in the telling, but the one I remember was how he rode through part of France on his horse, searching in vain for the front line! In spiritual warfare, we need to ask the crucial question, 'Where is the essential battle being fought? Where is the front line?' The biblical answer is, 'In the place of believing prayer'. Do you recollect the story of Exodus 17? It was Israel's first battle and the Amalekites had come against them in Rephidim. Moses did the most extraordinary thing for a leader: he left the battlefield and gave the leadership to young Joshua. With Aaron and Hur, he climbed the nearest hill and lifted up his arms in prayer to God. The fortunes of the battle changed backwards and forwards; now Israel prevailed and now Amalek overcame them. Then the truth transpired: when Moses lifted up his hands, Israel prevailed, and when Moses let down his hands, Amalek prevailed. The front line of the battle, and the issue of the day, they discovered, lay not with the fighters on the field, but with the intercessor on the mountain top (*Exod.* 17:8-15). That is why the strength of a church can only be measured by its prayer meeting.

Now the common reaction to this truth is to say, 'Yes, of course we know that prayer is terribly important, but let's be balanced. There are so many other things we have to do besides pray!' I must immediately agree. There *are*. But I am bound to tell you that over more than fifty years in the pastoral ministry, my conclusion is that, by and large, we are *good* at these other things; while in the really serious work of prayer we have to confess, most of us, that we are amateurs. And the place where we are mostly amateur is in the realm of having our priorities settled before God.

## THE PRIORITY OF THE MINISTRY OF THE WORD

That is the other key note of Acts 6:4: 'We will give ourselves to prayer and to the ministry of the word.' Let me just point out to you briefly the connection between the two. If you were to ask me, what is the key factor in learning to pray, I would have to answer, 'Increasing in the knowledge of God'. And if you pressed me to tell you where that was most likely to happen, I would have to answer, 'It is in his Word that God primarily reveals himself to us and that is where we come to know him better.' That is the great connection between prayer and preaching. The result of great preaching should not be the cry 'What a man!', but 'What a God!'

The other side of this truth is that it is prayer which opens the truth to us as it is preached, and illumines our understanding to see it in all its glory. I well remember Professor Finlayson of the Free Church College in Edinburgh, saying at a conference I attended as a young minister, 'There is nothing a Bible preaching pastor needs so much as a faithful, praying people, however few they may be.'

So let me ask you as we are called to battle in the twenty-first century, 'Have you found the front line yet, and are you engaged in the battle there?'

# 7

# THE PRAYER-LIFE OF PAUL

*For this reason, ever since I heard about your faith in the Lord*
*Jesus and your love for all the saints, I have not stopped giving*
*thanks for you, remembering you in my prayers. I keep asking*
*that the God of our Lord Jesus Christ, the glorious Father, may*
*give you the Spirit of wisdom and revelation, so that you may*
*know him better. I pray also that the eyes of your heart may*
*be enlightened in order that you may know the hope to which*
*he has called you, the riches of his glorious inheritance in the*
*saints, and his incomparably great power for us who believe.*
*That power is like the working of his mighty strength, which he*
*exerted in Christ, when he raised him from the dead, and seated*
*him at his right hand in the heavenly realms, far above all rule*
*and authority, power and dominion, and every title that can be*
*given, not only in the present age, but also in the one to come.*
*And God placed all things under his feet and appointed him to*
*be head over everything for the church, which is his body, the*
*fullness of him who fills everything in every way.*

EPHESIANS 1:15-23

I F I WERE ASKED what were the two dominant features of
the Apostle Paul's ministry, I would have little hesitation
in responding, 'Prayer and preaching'. I would put them in
that order, because it is the order of the apostolic priorities in
Acts 6:4, where the apostles resolve, 'We will give ourselves to
prayer and the ministry of the word.' But I think it may be the
order Paul would have chosen himself.

Of course it is very obvious that Paul was under a special constraint to preach: 'Woe to me if I do not preach the gospel!', he exclaims to the Corinthians in 1 Corinthians 9:16. However, it is perhaps less obvious to many of us that 'Paul's whole ministry was grounded in and developed from prayer', as the Professor of New Testament at Trinity Evangelical Divinity School has written.[1] So many of his epistles have the meat of gospel truth sandwiched between an assurance that he prays without ceasing for those to whom he writes, and an appeal to them to pray for him. For example, in Romans 1:9-10 Paul writes, 'God is my witness how constantly I remember you in my prayers at all times'. Then at the end of the letter, he appeals to them, 'I urge you brothers, by our Lord Jesus Christ and by the love of the Spirit, to join me in my struggle by praying to God for me' (*Rom.* 15:30).

Nowhere does Paul reveal himself as the great intercessor so movingly as in his letter to his fellow Christians at Ephesus, and I invite you now to listen with me to Paul's prayer in Ephesians 1:15-23.

> For this reason, ever since I heard about your faith in the Lord Jesus and your love for all the saints, I have not stopped giving thanks for you, remembering you in my prayers. I keep asking that the God of our Lord Jesus Christ, the glorious Father, may give you the Spirit of wisdom and revelation, so that you may know him better. I pray also that the eyes of your heart may be enlightened in order that you may know the hope to which he has called you, the riches of his glorious inheritance in the saints, and his incomparably great power for us who believe. That power is like the working of his mighty strength, which he exerted in Christ, when he raised him from the dead, and seated him at his right hand in the heavenly realms, far

[1] W. Bingham Hunter, *Dictionary of Paul and his Letters* (Downers Grove, IL: IVP, 1993), p. 725.

above all rule and authority, power and dominion, and every title that can be given, not only in the present age, but also in the one to come. And God placed all things under his feet and appointed him to be head over everything for the church, which is his body, the fullness of him who fills everything in every way.

While we would all have some reluctance to examine anyone else's prayer, I think it could be helpful to learn from Paul's prayer, thinking about why he prays, how he prays, and what he prays for.

## WHY PAUL PRAYS

Firstly, he has a deep desire to thank and praise God for the gospel. The phrase 'For this reason', at the beginning of verse 15, gives us the first key to the motives of Paul's praying as he does. The phrase refers back to the first half of the chapter where Paul is prompted to bow down in wonder and worship at the sheer glory of the salvation he has been expounding in verses 1-14. Specifically he is filled with gratitude to God that the Ephesians have been 'included in Christ' (verse 13), and for the evidence he sees in their lives of two things: faith in the Lord Jesus, and love for all the saints. In other words, he sees the evidences of grace—a right relationship with the Lord Jesus Christ, and a right relationship with their fellow believers. Having seen that, Paul is now motivated to bow before God in thanksgiving for the mighty work of grace that has been accomplished in them. It is his profound understanding of the Gospel which, as we often say, 'drives him to his knees'. I am prompted to ask myself how often recently I have been 'driven to my knees' by a similar desire to praise and thank God for the power and glory of the gospel. Paul says in verse 16, 'I have not stopped giving thanks'.

Secondly, he has a deep concern for the spiritual growth of the Ephesian church. Although his heart is filled with thanksgiving, Paul is not complacent about the spiritual condition of the Christians at Ephesus. He immediately assures them at the end of verse 16 of his remembrance of them in his prayers. H.C.G. Moule comments, 'How much of the Apostle's work for his converts consisted in the holy labour of special intercessory prayer'. It is a wonderful privilege to pray people *in* to the kingdom and to see God open their hearts to Christ. But it is no less wonderful to be used by God to pray someone *on* to maturity in Christ, and to see them grow in grace. Paul tells the Ephesians at the end of verse 17 that the deep burden in his heart for them is 'that you may know him better'. That is why he prays for them as he does.

## HOW PAUL PRAYS

We now turn to the manner of Paul's praying. The first thing to notice is that he prays with perseverance and persistence. Look at the first sentences in verse 16 and 17: 'I have not stopped giving thanks' and 'I keep asking'. In other words, his praying is not spasmodic or crisis praying, or praying which is controlled by his feelings. He emphasises this even more in chapter 6 verse 18: 'Pray in the Spirit on all occasions with all kinds of prayers and requests. With this in mind, be alert and always keep on praying for all the saints'. John Calvin reminds us that perseverance is God's singular gift.[1] How often have you prayed for that gift from God? And especially in relation to prayer?

Secondly, he prays focussed on 'the God of our Lord Jesus Christ, the glorious Father'. This concentration of Paul's mind on the being and character and glory of God dominates the whole of this first chapter of Ephesians. Verses 6, 12 and 14 all have the same phrase, 'to the praise of his glory', and it is a keynote not only of the profound

---

[1] Cf. John Calvin, *Commentary on the Book of the Prophet Ezekiel*, Vol. 1 (Edinburgh: Calvin Translation Society, 1849), p. 380.

theology of the first part of the chapter, but also of Paul's prayer. The truth to which this emphasis points is that the greatness and glory of God is the proper focus of all true prayer. Both creation and salvation are exclusively his work. The priority of prayer in all Christian thinking is a direct and logical result of this conviction. Let me illustrate. If salvation is all of God, then where should we direct our requests to see a true work of salvation? The only answer is 'to God'. If salvation is all of God, to whom do we give all the praise and glory when we see evidence of it? The only answer is 'to God alone'. This is why Paul says in verse 17 that he prays to 'the Father of glory'. This is why in verse 20 and 21, he sees Christ as exalted 'far above all rule and authority, power and dominion and every title that can be given, not only in the present age, but also in the one to come'. When I was a very young Christian, I remember a godly minister saying to me when we spoke about prayer, 'What makes all the difference in how you pray is the vision you have of God in all his glory'. That is certainly the root from which Paul's prayer life grew. It will not be otherwise for any of us. We now come to the third aspect of Paul's prayer:

## WHAT PAUL PRAYS FOR

There are three main petitions in this prayer in Ephesians 1. He prays for an increase in their knowledge of God. 'I keep asking that God… may give you the Spirit of wisdom and revelation, so that you may know him better' (verse 17). Do you remember the remarkable words of Jesus in John 17? 'This is eternal life: that they might know you, the only true God, and Jesus Christ whom you have sent'. Paul expresses the deepest desire of his life in these terms—'I want to know Christ'; 'I consider everything a loss compared to the surpassing greatness of knowing Christ Jesus my Lord' (*Phil.* 3:8-10).

I am troubled by the restricted way we speak of church growth today. It is almost always confined to *numerical* growth, whereas *spiritual growth* is scarcely mentioned. Now of course the New Testament gladly records for us the good news of numbers being added to the church, but the mere multiplying of under-developed 'babes in Christ', who have little depth in their understanding or maturity in the quality of their lives brings no glory to God. Paul sets out his 'mission statement' in Colossians 1:28: 'We proclaim him, admonishing and teaching everyone with all wisdom so that we may present every man mature in Christ'. The attributes of childhood are entirely acceptable, both in the physical and spiritual spheres, during childhood. But when they are prolonged into adulthood that is nothing less than a tragedy. So he prays in this paragraph 'that you may know him better'.

The whole idea of 'knowing God' is not a static but a dynamic concept. When someone asks you 'Do you know so-and-so?', you would normally reply in terms of *degrees* of knowledge—'I know him by name but not personally', or 'I know him a little but not intimately', or 'Of course I know him: he's my father!' This is why in the New Testament growing in grace and growing in the knowledge of the Lord Jesus Christ are linked together (see the last verse of 2 Peter). Since God is infinite and eternal and the psalmist tells us 'his greatness is unsearchable', we will never come to an end of knowing him until our knowledge is perfected in heaven (*1 Cor.* 13:12: 'Now I know in part; then I shall know fully, even as I am fully known'). Until that day, we need to give ourselves, like Paul, to praying for one another, that we might grow to know him better.

Secondly, he prays for their understanding of the call of God (verse 18). One of the great longings of the apostle is that the believers in Ephesus might have their hearts set not on earthly treasure, but on heavenly glory. That is what God has *called* us to, as Paul reminds us in Philippians 3:14: 'God has called me heavenward in Christ Jesus'. Here in Ephesians 1:18 he prays 'that you may know the hope to which he has called you, the riches of his glorious inheritance in the saints'. This is the dimension of salvation we too readily ignore or underplay. We are not just saved by grace through Christ; we are saved in hope, and that hope is not the secular 'hope' of something that is scarcely likely to happen ('I hope we may have a bright, warm, sunny day tomorrow'). It is a sure and certain hope: a guarantee from a God who cannot lie. It is obviously a matter of great importance to Paul that God might enlighten the hearts of the Ephesians, that they may grasp the nature of their heavenly inheritance, which Peter describes as 'imperishable, undefiled and unfading' in 1 Peter 1:4. Ultimately the great difference between the believer and the unbeliever is that for the former the best is yet to be, while for the latter the worst is yet to come. The Puritans spoke much of 'heavenly-mindedness' and it is undoubtedly the Bible's perspective on life that the Christian's true home and ultimate treasure is in heaven with Christ. Here we are forever 'strangers and pilgrims'. In this present life, there is always a 'not yet' for the child of God. That is why John reminds us in 1 John 3:2-3: 'Dear friends, now we are children of God, and what we will be has not yet been made known. But we know that when he appears, we shall be like him, for we shall see him as he is. Everyone who has this hope in him purifies himself, just as he is pure'.

Thirdly, He prays that they may understand something of the power of God (verses 19-23). Paul prays that his fellow believers in Ephesus may have a spiritual eye-opener, or a revelation, of what he calls God's 'incomparably great power'. What that means of course is that there is nothing anywhere in the universe which can be compared with the power of God. For us, it is therefore indescribable, unfathomable, and even unthinkable. What is even further beyond our understanding is for whom this power is exercised. Did you notice that in verse 19? It is 'for us who believe'. Now there is an idea for weak and needy believers to chew over! We do greatly need to plead with God to open the eyes of our understanding and convince us of the amazing, incomparable power of God which he exercises on behalf of his own children. Praying people in the Old Testament take hold of this truth in the way that Jeremiah does in chapter 32 of his prophecy and pray like this: 'Ah, Sovereign Lord, you have made the heavens and the earth by your great power and outstretched arm'. Then Jeremiah draws the obvious conclusion, 'Nothing is too hard for you' (verse 17). That ought to be our deepest conviction, especially since Paul goes on to provide us with an illustration of the power of God besides creation. We might ask where the power of God is supremely demonstrated, and the answer would be in verse 19 of Ephesians 1: 'That power is like the working of his mighty strength, which he exerted in Christ when he raised him from the dead, and seated him at his right hand in the heavenly realms, far above all rule and authority, power and dominion, not only in the present age, but also in the one to come'.

Do you see now why the literal, physical resurrection of Jesus lies at the heart of the Christian revelation? It is here above everywhere that we see God's demonstration of his incomparable power. It is here too that we see what has happened to us who have believed: the same divine energy which brought Christ from the grave has been at work in us when we were 'dead in trespasses and sins' to make us alive in Christ. Beloved, we have not just been convinced of gospel truth, won over by gospel love, and drawn to repentance and faith by gospel grace. We have been resurrected by gospel power to become new creatures in Christ Jesus.

It is this kingly Saviour whom God has set as head over the church (verse 22). No wonder Paul feels it incumbent upon him to pray that that church might grow and mature into everything God has called its people to be. May God give us a similar burden for the church in the twenty-first century.

# 8

# THE PRAYER OF
# A PENITENT SINNER

PSALM 51 IS THE FOURTH of what are often called 'The Penitential Psalms'. The others are Psalms 6, 32, 38, 102, 130 and 143. They are all heart-felt prayers to God for mercy in dealing with the psalmist's sin. They are psalms of contrition and confession, where the psalmist is freshly appalled by his sin, and conscious that his only hope lies in the miracle of God's mercy. For this reason, Luther called four of these psalms 'The Pauline Psalms'. He explains that when a man is bowed down by a deep awareness of his own sin, the language of his soul is the language of the psalmist, and it is also the language of the Apostle too as Paul focuses on justification by grace alone, in Christ alone and through faith alone. That is the ground on which all sinners must approach God. Whether our sin is the same as David's or not, Psalm 51 is a wonderful example of how the broken-hearted penitent should approach God, and find his mercy and his restoring grace.

The story of David's sin is told in 2 Samuel chapters 11 and 12. It is the story of a weak will, which fell before temptation, and of a scheming mind which, as it seemed, successfully covered over the sin. But into that situation, there came a searing, exposing word from God through Nathan the prophet. He had told David a story of a rich and powerful man with flocks and herds in abundance, who stole the lamb of a poor man who had nothing, in order to give hospitality to a visitor. David was infuriated at the idea and said, 'The man who did this deserves to die'. Nathan's response was 'You are that man'. David lay broken-hearted before God. Psalm 51 is his penitential cry, and it touches upon five subjects: mercy, cleansing, sin, forgiveness, and restoration. When we are dealing with God concerning our sin and failure, we need to confront each of these realities.

## MERCY

I never tire of reminding myself and others that the Psalms are not primarily theological treatises prepared in an ivory tower. They are the outpourings of the heart of a believer who is dealing with God about the deepest things in his life. In this case David is agonised by guilt and regret and shame - the aftermath of sin that has been exposed. It is significant that his first words are a cry for mercy from God. I once heard someone pray at a prayer meeting, 'We claim your mercy Lord'. It may have been an unthinking moment, but of course we have no claim on God's mercy. We may only beg for it as sinners who deserve nothing but God's judgment. And yet David appeals to God's covenant love, 'Have mercy on me O God, according to your steadfast love'. Do you notice that he is using the same language as the language of the Prodigal Son? 'Father, I am no more worthy to be called your son'. But like the prodigal, he is leaning on the truth that although sin may destroy our fellowship with God, it cannot remove our relationship with him. He still belongs to the covenant people of God, and nothing can change that. He therefore is able to appeal to 'your great compassion' (verse 1b), and God is still 'the God of my salvation' (verse 14a).

## SIN

Sin has a multiple vocabulary in the Bible, and David employs all the main words to describe what has gone wrong in his life. 'Transgression' (verse 1) is the outward, public act of breaking

God's law; 'iniquity' (verses 2 and 9) goes deeper: it is the inward condition and refers to the corruption of our character; the word 'sin' itself (verses 2 and 9) means literally 'to miss the mark', and has links with the archer's aiming at a target. If he misses the bull's eye, it does not really matter how widely or how narrowly he misses; he has failed to do what was required of him, and the result is the same. He has failed to reach God's standard. Understanding this should save us from excusing ourselves by 'comparing ourselves among ourselves', and being content with 'not being as bad as others'. But David's deepest insight about his sin, and the truth which focuses his penitence is in verse 4 where he cries out, 'Against you, you only have I sinned, and done this evil in your sight'. Now our first reaction to that cry might be that it is scarcely true. Surely he has sinned against Bathsheba, Uriah her husband, the unborn child, and so on. But the essence of his sin lies precisely where he had put his finger. It is in his personal rebellion which has its roots in a wilful self which has risen up against the Lord of glory, and proudly defied him.

It was in the most unlikely place and from the least expected people that I once was taught a lesson about this. I was standing in a newsagent's shop waiting to buy my morning newspaper. A little boy who was accompanying his father was exploring what was for sale on the shelves, and creating some havoc. The father remonstrated with him and told him to stop. To my amazement, the boy stood upright for a moment, faced his father and said, 'O, get lost'. Throughout the shop there were gasps of astonishment. I can only tell you that as I walked out into the street I was immediately struck by the fact that that was exactly what I was saying to God every time I defied his will, and it greatly sobered me. Mind you, David recognises in the psalm that the root of his sin does not lie in a sudden rebellion. In verse 5 he confesses that he was born with an innate corruption. Like the rest of us, he was born with a destiny to love and serve God, and an inclination to love and serve himself.

## CLEANSING

In verses 2 and 7 David discovers afresh that sin not only brings us under judgment, altering our position before God. It pollutes our nature, altering our condition before him. So David now pleads for the cleansing of his inner being, 'Wash me thoroughly from my iniquity, and cleanse me from my sin'. The Hebrew language has two main words for washing. One is what we might call 'a light rinse'. The other has the idea of 'pummelling', or removing ingrained dirt by a heavy laundering. It is this second word David uses here, recognising his need for a radical cleansing. Just how transforming God's cleansing is, you can see in verse 7b. 'Whiter than snow' is an intriguing phrase. If you have ever seen a bottle of milk on a snow-laden step, you will know what David means. There is nothing whiter than snow. 'Whiter than white' is what God intends for sin-blackened hearts, and so he calls his sinning people to him with these amazing words in Isaiah 1:18 'Come now let us reason together, says the Lord, though your sins are like scarlet, they shall be as white as snow'. The grace of God brings the fullest, deepest cleansing.

## FORGIVENESS

Just as sin is essentially rebellion against God, so true forgiveness comes from God alone, which is why Augustus Toplady teaches us to sing 'Thou must save and thou alone'. So David's deepest burden is not whether any human being is ready to blot out the memory of his sin, but whether God is willing to do so. So in verse 9 he prays, 'Hide your face from my sins, and blot out all my iniquity'. What a bold request! Here we touch upon the mystery and miracle of the grace of God, which Paul expounds for us in

Colossians 2:13ff: 'He forgave us all our sins, having cancelled the written code that was against us and that stood opposed to us; he took it away, nailing it to the Cross'. Perhaps most amazing of all, he has blotted our sins out of his memory as Hebrews 8:12 reminds us, 'I will remember their sins no more'. Do you grasp the full meaning of that? It means that when we come to the God of our salvation with a broken heart, mourning over a past sin, he asks 'What sin was that? And when was it? I don't remember it'. He has hidden his face from our sins and blotted them out of his memory.

## RESTORATION

Contrary to Satan's lies, sin always brings loss, not gain. The first thing David has become aware of losing is the joy of true fellowship with God (verse 8a). Instead of this he feels as if he is crushed and bruised under God's chastening hand (verse 8b). So he brings to God his deep need of healing from all the ravages of sin. This is one of the hallmarks of true repentance. The penitent sinner longs to be restored to God in the deepest places of his heart, and so he asks, 'Create in me a clean heart o God, and renew a right spirit within me'. It is of great significance that David uses the same word for 'create', which we find in Genesis 1:1 for the creation of the heavens and the earth. No more can mere man give himself a clean heart than he can create the heavens and the earth. This word in the Bible is exclusively used with God as its subject. But it is wonderful to contemplate the truth that the same God who formed the universe is again at work in the new creation to make us *not* reformed characters, but new creatures (*2 Cor.* 5:17).

The restoration of God is not just a restoration to his presence (verse 11) and fellowship (verse 12), but a restoration to usefulness and service (verse 13). But notice in verses 14 to 17, that David wants most to be restored to the highest of his privileges. What is that? It is the worship of God: 'My tongue will sing aloud of your righteousness. O Lord, open my lips and my mouth will declare your praise'. Notice, too, the restoration of the deepest longing of his heart - for the wellbeing of Zion and the restoration of the city of God (verse 18). But I would think that for David the greatest mystery of his restoration would be that through his ministry other sinners might return to God. The words 'restore' and 'return' in verses 12 and 13 derive from the same verb.

Derek Kidner, in his excellent commentary on the Psalms points out concerning Psalm 51 that 'the psalm itself is the richest answer to David's prayer, since it has shown generations of sinners the way home, long after they had thought themselves beyond recall." 'A broken and contrite heart, O God, you will not despise' (verse 17). Hallelujah!

---

' D. Kidner, *An Introduction and Commentary on Books I and II of the Psalms* (London: Inter-Varsity Press, 1973), p. 193.

# 9

# THIRSTING FOR GOD

*O God, you are my God, earnestly I seek you;*
*My soul thirsts for you, my body longs for you*
*In a dry and weary land where there is no water.*

PSALM 63:1

THERE ARE SEVERAL PSALMS which express in similar terms the psalmist's thirst for God, and it is this thirst which is our theme in this chapter. The relevance of 'thirsting for God' to the subject of prayer is similar to the relevance of hunger and appetite in relation to eating. We need to experience a true and deep desire for God before we will be drawn into his presence to have communion with him. For most people, I think the ultimate reason for prayerlessness is a lack of desire for God. I noted down in my notebook some time ago words I read in a book sent to me from America: 'It is a mark of spiritual barrenness in the church when people come to worship to fulfil a duty, rather than to satisfy an appetite'. And is it not true that so often this is our problem— the absence of a hunger, a thirst, an appetite for God? In the light of that, we should pray that God will speak to us through this psalm, and help us in this very important area of our lives.

As I read the words of the psalmist at the top of this page, I am driven to ask myself, as I suggest you ask yourself, 'Is that really the language of my soul before God? Does that express the things that lie in the deepest places of my heart?'

The Bible frequently speaks about thirst as a condition of the body which can be applied to the soul. In Psalm 42 we read, 'As the deer pants for streams of water, so my soul pants for you, O God. My soul thirsts for God, for the living God. When can I go and meet with God?' You find the same note in Psalm 143:6, 'I spread out my hands to you, my soul thirsts for you like a parched land'. And you find the prophets speaking the same language, for example in Isaiah chapter 55: 'Come, all you who are thirsty, come to the waters... come, buy and eat!' And the Lord Jesus Christ says in John 7:37, 'Let every one who thirsts come to me and drink'. It is the language of a physical experience, applied to a spiritual condition.

Of course, we are immediately in great difficulty in the western world, because there is hardly any of us who has experienced genuine thirst. We know almost nothing about having our lips parched, our tongues swollen and cleaving to the roof of our mouth, and our whole body dehydrated and racked with pain because of thirst. And the truth is, God help us, we know all too little about true spiritual thirst either.

It is certainly not true that we do not know thirst in the sense of a burning longing for things. In fact we thirst after all sorts of things. Some of them are just the tawdry toys of this passing world—things like material prosperity, or personal pleasure, or popularity, or power or position. Some are more sophisticated things to which we apply the word thirst. We speak about thirsting for knowledge, or for more aesthetic, nobler things like beauty. But seldom do we know what it is to thirst for God, and to be like the bride in the Song of Songs who cries through the streets, 'Have you seen him whom my soul loves?'. That is the thirst of which the psalmist writes. Will you join me, then, in asking some questions of this psalm?

## *WHAT EXACTLY IS THIS THIRST?*

The Psalmist's reply would I think be that it speaks of a deep, intense and all-consuming longing for God, for his fellowship, for his favour, for a felt sense of his presence. The spiritual reality, of which the physical experience is a symbol, is a blessed condition greatly to be coveted by God's people. This is why they take up this language when they are in a condition of true spiritual health. You find it in many of the hymns we sing: 'O for a heart to praise my God', 'O for a closer walk with God', 'Jesus, thou joy of loving hearts, thou fount of life, thou light of men, from the best bliss that earth imparts, we turn unfilled to thee again'.

## *WHAT ARE THE MARKS OF THIS THIRST?*

You will notice that there are several clearly described accompaniments of the thirst of which the psalmist speaks. The first of them is *urgency*. Look at verse 1: 'O God, you are my God, earnestly I seek you'. A number of translations have 'early I seek you', and that is the most literal translation of what the psalmist is saying. The idea of the dawn is contained in it. It is something that must be attended to at the first opportunity. It cannot be delayed or put aside. The man who is suffering from a raging thirst cannot be placated with words like, 'Well, there are so many other things to do: you will be attended to in good time'. There is an urgency about this thirst when it grips the soul of the child of God.

The second mark of it is *clarity*. That is, there is nothing vague about this longing in the psalmist's soul. It is not a vague desire for spiritual thrills. Of course there is a thirst which people experience in a state of unbelief rather than in a state of grace, and that is often very vague - a longing for happiness or peace or significance of some sort. But David has no such vagueness in his longings. He was in the desert of Judah the introduction tells us. But it is not his throne he wants back, or his comforts, or his position. It is God that he wants! Notice how that is clarified in what he says, 'O God, you are my God, earnestly I seek *you*; my soul thirsts for *you*, my body longs for *you*'. Notice that it is not blessing David seeks for: it is God.

The third mark of this thirst is *intensity*. Now of course we all know that there is an intensity which is unhealthy and leaves us less than well-balanced people. But this thirst is something which cannot be contained and confined to one area of life. It is something that absorbs the whole of a believer's being.

## WHERE DOES THIS THIRST COME FROM?

The first thing to say about that question is that such a thirst does not come from our fallen human nature. It is indeed an evidence of grace, and a work of saving grace. You will notice that at the very beginning of the psalm David says, 'O God, you are *my* God'. That is, he is speaking to the God who is already his God: he is in a state of grace, and this thirst is one of the gracious effects of a true work of grace. Thirst for milk is one of the first signs of physical life, and thirst for God is one of the earliest signs of spiritual life. One of the Puritans puts it in this way: 'Observe how it is with the new-born babe. He thirsts by the power of an irresistible instinct after his mother's milk, the destined food and nourishment of his infant life. Just so it is with the heaven-born soul and with the newborn, revived church. They thirst by the force of an irresistible spiritual instinct for God and his Word'.

In dead souls and dead churches there is nothing even approaching this thirst for God and his Word. But whenever someone is brought into a genuine state of grace, and whenever a church is awakened and people are converted to Jesus Christ, there will be this double thirst : a thirst for God and a desire for the Word of God, through which we come to know him more fully.

To press this matter further, in times when we are in a heightened state of grace (for example in days of revival) this thirst for God becomes more evident still. If you have read some of the history of revival, you will know that one of its characteristics is 'a people thirsting after God'. They do not need to be persuaded or cajoled into coming together to seek the face of God. There is a hunger for his presence and for his word. So in the Hebrides, for example, you read of fishing boats turning round and their crews making their way back to land and crowding into the church. Why? To seek God earnestly.

Now only God can produce that thirst, which is why it is so right to sing, 'Revive thy work, O Lord; *create* soul thirst for thee'.

## WHAT STIMULATES THIS THIRST FOR GOD?

You will notice that the psalmist tells us that this thirst is stimulated from the *past* (verse 2), from the *present* (verse 1), and from the *future* (verses 3-5).

First of all, he recalls his own experience in the past in verse 2: 'I have seen you in the sanctuary, and beheld your power and glory'. Memory is a great gift from God, especially when it enables us to recollect high occasions in our past experience when we have gazed upon the beauty and glory of God in his sanctuary. Here the psalmist recollects the blessings he has known while engaged in public worship. That of course is one of God's primary purposes in assembling his people together, that he might display his glory. So the thought of John Newton's hymn should be uppermost in our minds as we come to worship:

> Now gracious God Thine arm reveal,
> And make Thy glory known,
> Now let us all Thy presence feel,
> And soften hearts of stone.

Most of us who have been believers for a number of years can look back on such occasions. They were not just times of blessing for David *then*, but the memory of them captivates his soul *now* when he is in a dry and thirsty land.

Secondly, this thirst is stimulated from his present circumstances: he is in a dry and weary land, where there is no water (verse 1). He is cast out from his own home and city, and from the household of God's people. The desert of Judah has become a symbol for him of the situation in which he finds himself. And yet, he is thirsting for God more than for water. Does it ever occur to you that God may deprive his children of the means of grace to give them an appetite for himself?

Many years ago, I had the privilege of a visiting an unusually godly man who was very ill and in hospital in Scotland. For some time he had been confined to home and to bed and had now been in hospital for several weeks. As we talked, he said something to me I have never forgotten: 'I have greatly valued my private communion with the Lord during these difficult days, but never again will I take for granted the special blessing of public worship. I think I understand what the psalmist meant when he said, "How amiable are thy tabernacles, O Lord of hosts. My soul longeth, yea, even fainteth for the courts of the Lord: my heart and my flesh crieth out for the living God". I could only say that I have a deeper longing for him than ever'. As I left the hospital, it occurred to me that before too long he would be worshipping with those of whom Revelation 7:16 says, 'They shall hunger no more, neither thirst any more'.

Thirdly, his thirst is stimulated by his future prospects, as you will see in verses 3 to 5. The power and glory and love of God have given him an assurance that he will not thirst in vain. Verse 3 and 4 concentrate on the future 'My lips will glorify you', 'I will praise you as long as I live', 'My soul will be satisfied as with the richest of foods'. His thirst is excited by the promises of a gracious and faithful God, and he trusts him to fulfil his promise as does the psalmist in Psalms 42 and 43, 'Put your hope in God, for I shall yet praise him, my Saviour and my God'.

Before closing this chapter, let me pass on to you some words which I have myself found helpful. I should think that in all our minds, there is the question, 'How can this thirst for God grow in an ordinary believer like me?' These are the words of a sixteenth century French Benedictine monk called François Rabelais. He said, 'The appetite grows with eating.' Of course we all prove the truth of that simple saying physically: as we eat more, our appetite increases. And the converse is also true: the less we eat, the more our appetite shrinks. There is a parallel in the spiritual sphere. The more we feed our souls on God's word, the more our desire for him will grow. I think that is one of the things in Isaiah's mind when he says in that great invitation to the thirsty in chapter 55: 'Listen, listen to me and eat what is good, and your soul will delight in the richest of fare'.

One of the fearful things about depriving yourself of the Bread of Life is that your appetite slackens. But the appetite grows with eating as you feed your soul on the Word of God. Do not be deceived into thinking that there is some mystic formula for knowing an increasing thirst for God. The God-given way is by feeding on his Word. As you drink deeply there of the wells of salvation, you will find yourself saying, 'I hunger and I thirst; Jesus my manna be'.

As we too live in a dry and thirsty land, both in the church and in the world, I believe there are few things the living God longs to hear more from his people than the cry, 'O God, you are my God, earnestly I seek you; my soul thirsts for you, my body longs for you'. God grant us such times of refreshing.

## 10

# THE INTERCESSORY MINISTRY OF THE HOLY SPIRIT

*In the same way, the Spirit helps us in our weakness. We do not know what we ought to pray for, but the Spirit himself intercedes for us with groans that words cannot express. And he who searches our hearts knows the mind of the Spirit, because the Spirit intercedes for the saints in accordance with God's will.*

ROMANS 8:26-27

I HAVE OFTEN BEEN STRUCK BY the amazing lengths to which God goes in order to persuade his people to pray. He gives us examples in Scripture of the ministry of prayer in the lives of almost all his servants. Above all, he gives us the supreme example, allowing us to overhear the Lord Jesus Christ himself at prayer in the most intimate of circumstances in John 17, when he is within hours of his death. He presses invitations upon us, again and again, to 'wait on the Lord', to 'draw near to God', to 'call upon him while he is near'. But you may have noticed that possibly the most convincing evidence of how deeply God desires that we should learn to pray, is that all three persons of the Godhead—Father, Son and Holy Spirit—combine together to persuade us to take up the ministry of prayer.

First, God the Father invites and pleads with us to seek his face, and to draw near to him, often with a note of urgency—'Seek the Lord while he may be found; call upon him while he is near' (*Isa.* 55:6). These appeals are often strengthened by accompanying promises: 'Come near to God and he will come near to you' (*James* 4:8); 'You will seek me and find me when you seek me with all your heart' (*Jer.* 29:13).

Secondly, God the Son, by his sinbearing death on the cross opens a new and living way into the Father's presence for us. The glorious good news which comes from Calvary is, 'We have access to the Father'. Then when the Lord Jesus Christ ascends into heaven, we are told in Hebrews 7:25 that one of the ministries he is given there is to intercede for 'those who come to God through him', whereby he 'saves us to the uttermost'. Jesus' intercession is a key to our full salvation.

Thirdly, God the Holy Spirit, as the Spirit of sonship, teaches us to say 'Abba, Father' (*Rom.* 8:15). But that is only the beginning of his ministry. In Romans 8:26-27, Paul touches a new depth of this subject by describing for us the intercessory ministry of the Holy Spirit. This means that we have an Intercessor in heaven, the risen and exalted Christ, and we have a second divine Intercessor dwelling in our hearts—the person of the Holy Spirit.

It is to this remarkable ministry of the Holy Spirit that we will devote our attention in the rest of this chapter: first as to the need for it, and second as to the nature of it.

## THE NEED FOR THE HOLY SPIRIT'S INTERCESSION (Rom. 8:26)

This need is explained by Paul simply and briefly in verse 26—'The Spirit helps us in our weakness'. Now of course that is a reference to the fundamental condition of every man and woman. We are creatures, not the Creator. But there is another side to this condition: we are fallen creatures, and are born into this world with the inabilities and disabilities of fallen creatures. And it is important to remember that even redeemed men and women have the limitations of fallen creatures. 'We are saints, not angels', as William Still used to say.

Now in verse 26, Paul applies the problem of our native weakness to the most important sphere of our life—that is, to our praying. Here the manifestation of our weakness is, 'We do not know what we ought to pray for'. Let me just ask you to pause for a moment and remind yourself that Paul says 'we', not 'you'. In other words the great apostle includes himself in this confession of weakness, and he does so for our encouragement.

There are many illustrations in Scripture of God's people in this situation. For example, there is Moses in Deuteronomy 3:23-26, pleading with God to be allowed to go over to the land beyond the Jordan river. God responds in verse 26, 'Do not speak to me anymore about this matter'. He had asked for the wrong thing.

Or think of Paul himself in 2 Corinthians 12:1-10. He was experiencing great weakness and in that weakness he pleaded with the Lord to take away the thorn in his flesh. But God declined to do it and told him he had asked for the wrong thing.

I wonder if we might even hear a hint of this same weakness in the confession of our Lord Jesus Christ in the days of his flesh in John 12:27? 'Now is my soul troubled, and what shall I say? "Father save me from this hour?" No, it was for this very reason I came to this hour. Father glorify your name'. And in Gethsemane he actually asks, 'If it is possible, let this cup pass from me'. Leon Morris points out that there is no question of whether or not Jesus would do the Father's will. The question is, 'What was the Father's will?' Calvin wisely says, 'the human feelings from which Christ was not immune, were in him pure and free from sin'.[1]

Now before we come to the nature of the Spirit's intercessory ministry, we need to correct a false conclusion many people draw at this point. The false conclusion is that because we do not

[1] John Calvin, *Commentary on the Gospel According to John,* Vol. 2 (Edinburgh: Calvin Translation Society, 1847), p. 33.

know what we ought to pray for, we cannot pray, and we can end up asking, 'What is the point of trying to pray?'

The first answer to this is that prayer is an obligation for the Christian, not an option. It is a commandment which Jesus gives to his disciples—'Watch and pray' (*Matt.* 26:41); 'When you pray' (not 'if you pray', in Luke 11:2), and Paul puts it quite categorically: 'Men ought always to pray'. But recognising our weakness, God has given us his Holy Spirit, to take up residence in our hearts. This is what Paul is speaking of when he writes to the Ephesians, 'I pray that ... he may strengthen you with power through his Spirit in your inner being' (*Eph.* 3:16). He is going to explain just how the Holy Spirit strengthens us in these verses in Romans 8.

The second answer is that although our knowledge of God's will is limited, it is not non-existent. What is it that we do not know? It is not the moral will of God, for we do know that. God has revealed it to us in Scripture, and the Holy Spirit applies it to our conscience. A good example is in the Ten Commandments, which is the moral will of God for all his creatures.

Neither is it the spiritual will of God—that is, what God's spiritual purpose is for us. He wants us to grow in grace and in the knowledge of our Lord and Saviour Jesus Christ. He wants us to become more and more like Jesus. He wants us to be God-centred and Christ-centred, rather than self-centred. What is it then that we do *not* know?

Deuteronomy 29:29 gives us the answer: 'The secret things belong unto the Lord our God, but the things revealed belong to us and to our children for ever'. There are certain things which remain in the secret counsels of God which we shall never know, and we must be entirely content never to know them. However, there is normally enough of the will of God revealed and taught in Scripture for us to pray with complete assurance in all kinds of situations.

Thus far, we have thought about the need for the Holy Spirit's intercessory ministry. Now we must turn to the nature of the Holy Spirit's ministry.

## THE NATURE OF THE INTERCESSORY MINISTRY OF THE HOLY SPIRIT (*Rom.* 8:26-27)

Having confessed with Paul that 'we do not know what to pray for as we ought', we find the answer to that dilemma in the very next sentence—'but the Spirit himself intercedes for us with groans that words cannot express'. So when we are perplexed and indeed baffled as to what we should pray for, the Holy Spirit takes up our cause. And the vital thing about the Holy Spirit in this connection is that he has a perfect knowledge of the will of God (verse 27). That is of course what we would expect, since he is God, and therefore the 'mind of the Lord [that is, God]' (*Rom.* 11:34), 'the mind of Christ' (*1 Cor.* 2:16) and 'the mind of the Spirit' (*Rom.* 8:27) are all one and the same.

There are three matters identified in our text which help us to understand the nature of the Spirit's help:

The first is found in the word Paul uses for 'help'. The brief word in English is actually a lengthy and complex word in Greek, consisting of a string of smaller words meaning 'together with' or 'along with', 'for' or 'on behalf of', and the final word is 'bear' or 'carry'. So it describes what happens when you have too great a load to carry and someone comes and takes hold of one end of it.

It fits perfectly the idea that the Holy Spirit does not take over praying for you, and you, as it were, hand over the task to him. Instead, he enters into the task with you. You pray and the Spirit prays. That leads us to the second matter.

What is meant by the Spirit's 'groaning' in verse 26? Paul describes this groaning with an explanation—'groans that words cannot express', or groans 'that are too deep for words' (ESV).

Clearly it is the expression of desires and longings which cannot be put into human language. Calvin comments that Paul calls the groans into which we break forth by the impulse of the Spirit 'unutterable', because they far exceed the capacity of our intellect.[1] The question has often been raised in this connection, 'Is this groaning the believer's or the Holy Spirit's?' Calvin's answer seems to be that it is the believer under the impulse of the Holy Spirit, and neither the one without the other. Let me just ask you, 'Have you never found God the Holy Spirit taking you up in prayer, with longings which could not be expressed in human language? Have you not known times when something like a wordless groan is all that can escape your lips?' Note that although the groaning of which Paul speaks is inexpressible, it is not necessarily inaudible. Whether it is audible to human beings on earth or not, it is certainly heard and interpreted by God in heaven, as Paul now goes on to explain.

The third matter is how God responds to the Spirit's intercessory ministry in verse 27. Paul begins verse 27 by describing God as 'he who searches our hearts'. God declares in Jeremiah 17:10, 'I the Lord search the heart'. And in the context of Romans 8:27, when God searches the heart of the true believer, he finds the Holy Spirit at work there, interceding in prayer for us. Paul then goes on to say that the same God who searches our hearts 'knows the mind of the Spirit'. So God reads the mind of the Spirit who intercedes for the saints according to the will of God, and he finds prayer which is perfectly attuned to the will of God, both in content and intent.

Now we need to think about the implications of this truth. A minister friend of mine in America has two words mounted on his study desk. They are 'So what?'—He realises that this is precisely the question many of his hearers will be asking, for example when

---

[1] John Calvin, *Commentary on the Epistle to the Romans* (Edinburgh: Calvin Translation Society, 1849), p. 313.

they have reached this very point at which we have arrived in our study of Romans 8:26-27. What are the implications of this truth for ordinary Christian believers like ourselves? Let me suggest some conclusions we ought to draw:

The first is what Spurgeon is reputed to have said when he had preached on these same verses in Romans 8: 'I thank God that my prayers go to heaven in the revised version!' What Spurgeon was thanking God for was the ministry of the Intercessor who dwells in our hearts if we are true believers—the Holy Spirit of God.[1]

Secondly, we should never be discouraged from praying because we are perplexed about what we should ask God for in a particular situation. On the contrary we should come to the throne of grace with complete confidence in the knowledge, power and compassion of the Holy Spirit.

Thirdly, the relation we have with the Holy Spirit is one of faith, not mainly one of feeling. So we do not need to feel the help of the Holy Spirit's intercession in order to benefit from it. The same is true of Christ's intercession for us in heaven.

Fourthly, there is a tendency in some circles to take the wrong meaning from Paul's teaching and conclude that we do not need words in prayer and that in a sense the most spiritual prayers may just be sighs and groans. But when Jesus teaches the disciples to pray he says, 'When you pray, say...' and he gives them words for their lips to speak. The prophet Hosea is speaking for the whole Scripture when he says in Hosea 14, 'Take with you words, and turn to the Lord'.

Fifthly, this leads me to one final thing we need to have in mind in this connection. The context of these verses we have been considering is a chapter where Paul is deeply concerned for the unusual sufferings and trials of the Roman Christians.

---

[1] I have tried to source this Spurgeon quotation but without success!

It would simply be true to say that these circumstances are unusual and not normal. But we may all some day share the experience of our brothers and sisters in this chapter, and we need to know that we not only have an Intercessor in heaven, but one who dwells within our hearts who also intercedes for us to help our weakness in prayer. As one hymnwriter put it,

'Think what Spirit dwells within thee'.

## 11

# CORPORATE PRAYER

*Again, I tell you that if two of you on earth agree about anything you ask for, it will be done for you by my Father in heaven. For where two or three come together in my name, there am I with them.*

MATTHEW 18:19-20

PROBABLY MOST OF US THINK about prayer in terms of a solitary activity. That is not surprising, since Jesus is often depicted as withdrawing from all others, and seeking a secret place to commune with his Father: 'Immediately Jesus made the disciples get into the boat and go on ahead of him to the other side, while he dismissed the crowd. After he had dismissed them, he went up on a mountainside by himself to pray. When evening came, he was there alone' (*Matt.* 14:23). Again, he teaches us in the Lord's Prayer to 'Go into your room, close the door, and pray to your Father'. Private, personal prayer is therefore essential and not optional.

However, it is also vital for us to see the reason for these commands in Matthew chapter six and verse six. Jesus is contrasting true prayer with the prayers of the Pharisees who 'love to pray standing in the synagogues and on the street corners, to be seen of men'. They do this because they are hypocrites, acting a part, and three times over in Matthew chapter six, Jesus warns his disciples, 'Do not be like them'.

# PRAYER, A BIBLICAL PERSPECTIVE

On the other hand, at the very beginning of the Lord's Prayer, Jesus teaches us to pray not '*My* Father' but '*Our* Father'. In other words, he is teaching us to pray together. Indeed, he spells out the benefits of corporate prayer further on in Matthew's Gospel, in chapter 18, verses 19 and 20: 'Again, I tell you that if two of you on earth agree about anything you ask for, it will be done for you by my Father in heaven. For where two or three come together in my name, there am I with them.'

The balance of truth regarding solitary and corporate prayer in the Bible seems to be that no-one can engage in public prayer who does not know what it is to engage with God in private. But the man or woman who has begun to pray in private will gravitate to the fellowship of praying people in the church.

Perhaps you will forgive a personal illustration of this. I came to faith in a church in Glasgow where the minister, Dr William Fitch, taught us regularly from Scripture the central place of prayer in the life of the church. The church prayer meeting was held on Saturday evening. The evidence that someone had been converted to Christ in the congregation was that they would walk into the prayer meeting on a Saturday evening. That meeting became the power house, under God, for a remarkable work of grace in that church. The only reason a believer would be absent from it would be that they were either ill or away from home. Very properly, people called it the 'prayer fellowship', for that was where we experienced true Christian fellowship and mutual support at the deepest level.

In September 1981, Rev James Philip (a friend and mentor of many ministers like myself in Scotland) wrote in his pastoral letter to the congregation of Holyrood Abbey Church in Edinburgh, what he regarded as the essentials of a living church:

A ministry of the Word at depth, not merely in terms of the recovery of biblical exposition, but particularly in a determination to allow all the vital thrust of that Word to do its costly work in our lives, for the production of Christian character and wholeness; an incisive pastoral ministry, helping the Word home in personal application; the establishing of a life of corporate prayer as the powerhouse of the work and the battleground on which a significant advance in the work is made.

Clearly, the establishment of this corporate prayer ministry is something which matters to God, if we take seriously what he says to Solomon:

> If my people who are called by my name, will humble themselves and pray and seek my face, and turn from their wicked ways, then will I hear from heaven and will forgive their sin and will heal their land. Now my eyes will be open and my ears attentive to the prayers offered in this place (*2 Chron.* 7:14).

Of course these words apply to meetings for public worship, but historically it has been the special meeting convened for prayer and waiting on God which has been associated with times of spiritual renewal and the outpouring of God's Spirit upon churches and communities.

So when the spiritual state of the church is moribund and compromised and weak, that is when the people of God should heed this call of God—'If my people…'. When Satan is apparently triumphing in the world, that is when the church corporately needs to follow the example of the church in Acts chapter 12 and verse 5: 'Peter was kept in prison, but the church was earnestly praying to God for him.' Then Peter's chains fell off, iron gates burst open and the power of God triumphed over the enemy. When the work of the Gospel is being hindered by whatever means, that is the time for the people of God to follow the example so clearly displayed by the early church in Acts chapter four: 'Then they called Peter and John in again and commanded them not to speak or teach at all in the name of Jesus' (verse 18); 'After further threats, they let them go' (verse 21); 'On their release, Peter and John went back to their own people and reported all that the chief priests and elders had said to them. When they heard this, they raised their voices together in prayer to God. "Sovereign Lord" they said...' (verses 23 and 24); 'After they prayed, the place where they were meeting was shaken' (verse 31). This is the church's unique ministry. No other corporate activity will fulfil it. Nothing else is a substitute for it. So it is not surprising that Luther is reputed to have said, 'Pray in the Church, with the Church, for the Church'. Prayer is the duty of the church corporately, not just of Christians individually. Is it not then highly significant that in these days (I write in the year 2011) one of the chief marks of the church's malaise is the poverty of prayer meetings in the evangelical churches of the western world?

Finally, in connection with the theme of corporate prayer, let me direct your attention to a remarkable chapter in the Book of Revelation. It is the eighth chapter and especially the first five verses, which I have sometimes entitled, 'What Happens After We Pray?'

You may know that this is the chapter in Revelation where the seventh seal is opened by the Lamb. When it was opened there was silence in heaven for about half an hour (verse 1). That silence was a great contrast to what we read about in the previous paragraphs. There we are told of a multitude which no one could number who cried out with a loud voice: 'Salvation belongs to our God who sits on the throne and to the Lamb' (*Rev.* 7:10). Now at the beginning of chapter eight, God appears to be saying 'Shhh; quiet!', and the colossal noise is replaced by a total silence. We inevitably ask, 'Why would God require silence in heaven?' It is obviously linked with what we are told in verse three, where an angel is given a golden censer, filled with incense (often associated with prayer in Scripture) and the prayers of the saints, and he carries them up to the very throne of God. Now God silences everything, so that he can hear the prayers of the saints. Leon Morris points out that 'John means us to see that the prayers of God's people are supremely important.'[1] What happens after we pray? Well, God concentrates heaven's attention on the cries which ascend from his people to his throne. Of course, the world would dismiss as insignificant these small groups of people pleading with God, but in God's eyes, these are the most important people on earth, and the most significant events taking place in the universe. The real question is, 'Where are the great decisions of our times being taken?' The answer of the Book of Revelation is not in the conferences of the great powers on earth, but at the throne of the Sovereign Lord of the universe. And that means that the prayers of the saints are crucial to the events of our times.

Let me quote to you some words written by Professor T. F. Torrance, late of Edinburgh University. He is commenting on this very chapter of Revelation:

> The prayers of the saints and the fire of God move the whole course of the world. They are the most potent, the most disturbing, the most revolutionary, the most terrifying powers that the world knows. Would to God that we in Christ's church really understood the power of prayer like that! It is through prayer that the Spirit of God comes upon the Church in tongues of fire. It is through prayer that Satan falls like lightning to the ground. It is through prayer that the Voice of the Gospel thunders through the clouds of darkness.[2]

May God have mercy on his church, and teach us where ultimate power lies.

---

[1] Leon Morris, *Revelation: An Introduction and Commentary* (London: Tyndale Press, 1969), p. 120.
[2] T. F. Torrance, *The Apocalypse Today* (London: James Clarke, 1960), pp. 73-74.

# 12

# COMMON DIFFICULTIES

I DO NOT KNOW ANY HONEST Christian who has no difficulties with regard to prayer. Nor do I know any Christian who believes he or she has all the answers to these problems. However, it is important to try to think them through in the light of the teaching of Scripture, which is our only infallible guide.

Such problems can usually be divided into three groups: theological difficulties; spiritual difficulties; and practical difficulties. It is my hope to deal with them under these headings, and I should explain that these are the questions which people have asked about, during fifty years in the pastoral ministry!

## THEOLOGICAL DIFFICULTIES

1. *'If God is all-powerful, all-wise, and all- loving, and knows the needs of his children perfectly, why does he insist that we must ask him for what we need?'*

The first thing is that it is not really accurate to say that God insists that we must ask for what we need. In fact he gives us daily multiple blessings for which we have never asked, nor do we even recognise the source from which they have come.

The second thing to say is that if we are Christians, we are in a relationship with God by adoption and regeneration—we are his children and he is our Father. Now as a loving Father, God delights to be entreated by his children. So Jesus teaches us to 'ask', 'seek' and 'knock'. Significantly, God's only begotten Son, the Lord Jesus

Christ, is told by God to ask for his inheritance in Psalm 2:8. This asking involves the exercise of faith, which is the essence of our relationship with God: a childlike trust in him.

The third thing we need to say is that the prayer of faith is the God-ordained means by which his perfect will comes to pass. The prayers of his people are part of the process by which his will is done on earth. So Jesus teaches us to pray, 'Thy will be done'.

2. *'Does prayer change God's mind?'*

No. Read Numbers 23:19, where God puts these words into the mouth of Balaam: 'God is not a man that he should lie, nor a son of man that he should change his mind. Does he speak and then not act? Does he promise and then not fulfil?' So prayer is not a means of bending God's will to ours. Prayer is rather a means of seeing God's will put into action. It should also be a means of changing our will to conform to the will of God. The pattern for this is in Gethsemane, when Jesus in prayer asked that 'the cup' might pass from him, but added, 'But not my will but yours be done'. The Bible also speaks about 'striving' or 'wrestling' in prayer. It is in prayer that we defeat the designs of Satan to frustrate the will of God, and restrain him. So Paul urges the church at Rome to 'join me in my struggle by praying to God for me' (*Rom.* 15:30). You can see the nature of this battle in which we are involved: it is the battle between Christ, who says in words recorded in Hebrews 10:9, 'I am come to do your will', and Satan whose purpose is to oppose God's word and will. This battle began in the Garden of Eden and continues in the believer's life as we pray, 'Your will be done on earth as it is in heaven'. The believer's desire is not to see the will of God changed, but to see it fully done.

3. *'Does God always answer prayer?'*

If that question really means, 'Does God always give me what I want?', I would have to respond, 'No, I thank God with all my heart that he doesn't!' When I recollect some of the things I have genu-inely wanted God to do, or give me, I want to say with Spurgeon, 'I thank God my prayers go to heaven in the Revised Version.' But if the question means, 'Does God always hear my prayer and re-spond to it?', the answer is an unequivocal, 'Yes'. However, when an earthly father says 'no' to his child's request, it is not because he did not hear the petition, nor because he does not care about his child. It may be precisely because he cares so much and understands the implications in a way that the child does not, that he says 'no'. The other possibility is that he is able to discern the future as the child cannot, and he says, 'Not just now, probably later, but this is not the best moment to give you this or that.' In that case, we are to 'wait patiently for the Lord' as the psalmist tells us he did in Psalm 40:1. We are living in an 'instant' age, and are not very good at patience, but it is a fruit of the Spirit which we need to ask God to cultivate in our hearts. One form of it is persevering in prayer, which is the theme of Jesus' parable in Luke chapter 11. There is one other matter which requires comment in connection with unanswered prayer. It is the issue of our motive as we pray. James tells us in his letter (*James* 4:3) that we may ask and not receive 'because you ask with wrong motives'. So, as we come to God, we need to ask him to purify the motives that lie deep in our hearts, and confess and forsake those which grieve him.

4. '*If prayer is so important, why does God not make it easy, rather than so difficult?*'

It is true that God does sometimes give his people what has often been described as 'great liberty' in prayer. But we are not praying in a world of spiritual peace and quiet, but in a world of spiritual warfare and hostility. The enemy of God and of the Christian, the devil himself, knows the crucial importance of prayer. It is trite but true to say, 'Satan trembles when he sees, the weakest saint upon his knees.' I have no doubt that he deliberately opposes every occasion when a believer turns to wait upon God. When I was a young minister, I used to be astonished by the number of times the telephone rang, not so much when I began to study as when I began to pray! We find ourselves wrestling, not against flesh and blood, but against principalities and powers... and against the spiritual forces of evil in the heavenly realms (see *Eph.* 6:12-13). This is why any minister of the gospel will tell you that he is much more tired after praying than after preaching. However, we need to keep in mind that God has gone to great lengths to encourage us to pray: he has given us an example of prayer in Jesus' teaching and practice; he has given us the indwelling Holy Spirit who helps us (*Rom.* 8:26-27); he has given us the perfect intercessor at his right hand in heaven who never ceases to pray for us: he has given us his own commands and promises ('come near to God and he will come near to you' - *James* 4:8). Above all, at infinite cost he has opened a new and living way into his presence, so that we may have access to his throne (see *Heb.* 10:19-22).

5. '*Why does Jesus teach us to pray, "Lead us not into temptation, but deliver us from the evil one"? Would God ever lead his children into temptation?*'

Let me first of all point out that in this petition in the Lord's Prayer, we are recognising two things. First, our own great weakness and vulnerability in the face of the devil's attempts to entice us to sin. Second, God's complete sufficiency to deliver us.

The second thing to point out is that there are two meanings of the same biblical word: they are 'temptation' (in the sense of drawing us to sin) and 'testing' (in the sense of putting us through trial). James 1:13 tells us that God does not tempt anyone in the first sense, but in the same chapter in verse 2 he tells us to count it all joy when we face trials (same word) of many kinds. Now the same

God who will never entice us to sin (as the devil does) is in control of the devil himself. So when Job was experiencing Satanic temptation, we read in Job 1:12 that God restricts Satan's freedom as to how he will tempt Job—'on the man himself, do not lay a finger'.

The third thing to say is that when we are facing temptation and testing, we are all morally weak and therefore in danger. God may well use the devil's testing for our greater good, but we must constantly look to him to protect and keep us.

The final thing to point out is that there are two elements in temptation. There is the desire and the opportunity. Sometimes we have the desire but not the opportunity. Sometimes we have the opportunity but not the desire. But when both desire and opportunity coincide, then we are in the heart of the fires of temptation, and recognise how much we need to pray, 'Lead us not into temptation, but deliver us from the evil one.'

## SPIRITUAL DIFFICULTIES IN PRAYER

1. On several occasions people have asked me about a particular difficulty they have in relation to praying in a prayer meeting. The problem is really concerned with the motive behind our praying. It has been put to me like this: 'If I were absolutely honest, when I pray in a prayer meeting, I am often more concerned with what other people will think about my praying, than about what God thinks.' Let me first of all say in answer to this problem that none of us is immune from the temptation. Not only so, but it is true that we cannot ignore the other people who are present in a prayer meeting—we are, as it were, the spokesperson for the whole company before God. So we pray in the first person plural, not singular ('we' and not 'I'). We also pray for what will most likely occupy the hearts and minds of the others, as well as our own. But it is undoubtedly true that there is a temptation to try to impress other people

rather than to get through to God. Hypocrisy is bad anywhere, but worst in this situation. The New Testament word for 'hypocrite' is the Greek word for an 'actor', and it is a dreadful prostitution of praying to make it a vehicle for acting a part. Jesus warns us against it in Matthew 6:5. Only God can give us a pure heart when we pray, and we will of course plead with him to purify our motives before going to the prayer meeting. Further, I would suggest that the manner in which we pray should be with simple language, with a focussed object and preferably briefly. Some people have found their voice at a prayer meeting for the first time when they wrote out their prayer on a card, and read the words aloud at the prayer time.

2. Someone once said to me, 'I have read in Psalm 66:18, "*If I had cherished sin in my heart, the Lord would not have listened*". Does that mean that God only hears the prayers of the perfectly holy?'

My reply, if I remember, was, 'Thankfully, no.' When I was a young Christian, my minister said something to me which I wrote down: 'We pray as justified sinners, not as glorified saints.' We have access to God not because of anything we are or could ever become, but because Christ has opened 'a new and living way for us' (*Heb.* 10:20). In his atoning death he has taken all his own into the presence of his Father, and presents us faultless before him. But that faultlessness is not a moral accomplishment of our own but the divinely provided clothing of our salvation. God's throne is rightly called a throne of Grace. The last words of Psalm 66 are 'Praise be to God who has not rejected my prayer, or withheld his love from me.' However, it is important to add that persistent sin is a barrier between us and God, and it must be dealt with—first by confession (see *Psa.* 51) and then by repentance (see *Deut.* 4:29-31).

3. *'It sometimes seems as if persevering with the same prayer is like
pestering God to do what I want, rather than accepting that he
does not mean me to have what I am asking for'.*

I have lost count of the number of people who have asked me
some such question about persevering in prayer and how long one
should go on asking. Part of the answer lies, of course, in what it
is that you are asking for, and here again we need to seek the will
of God and nothing less. But I have a friend for whose salvation
someone prayed for twenty years, and he will be eternally grateful
that she did not give up. Again, two elderly ladies in the Island
of Lewis prayed for two years that God would come and visit the
island in revival, and believed it was God who gave them that burden and the faith to keep on asking. A dear friend of mine who is
now in glory was one of the early converts in that revival, and he
often expressed his gratitude to God for the faithfulness of these
old ladies.

However, it would be important to remember the example of
Paul in 2 Corinthians 12:8-9. He prayed repeatedly that his 'thorn
in the flesh' might be taken away, but God's answer was that he
should trust in the sufficiency of God's grace to enable him to live
with it. The vital thing is to be utterly committed to God's perfect
will.

## PRACTICAL DIFFICULTIES IN PRAYER

It may be that you do not have either theological or spiritual difficulties in relation to prayer, but you do have some simple
practical matters which hinder you. For example you may ask how
a young Christian should divide the time available to them, and
where and when they should pray. My own conviction is that it
is wise to begin with a shorter time and enlarge and expand it as
you grow spiritually. Let us say you can set aside half an hour in a
day. I would suggest you use the first ten minutes entering God's

presence, and worshipping him with the help of a psalm, reading a passage of Scripture, using some system which will take you through the Bible eventually. There are many bible reading notes which will help you to understand what you read, and apply it to your own life and circumstances. I would spend the next ten minutes praying the message of the passage into my own life: there may well be things God is speaking to me about through these verses. Then I would spend the last ten minutes going through the list of people I have in my prayer list, praying for each of the people named there alongside their needs. In the last few minutes I would commit my own day to the Lord and seek his blessing upon it. It is important regularly to review your prayer list and the way you use it . As to the time of day, just make sure you are not too tired. As to the place, some of us are fortunate enough to have a room of our own or some place where we will be undisturbed. Others are not, and need to use imagination and initiative. You can pray while you walk, or in a church building, at lunch time for example. As you grow as a Christian, of course, you will find you need more and more time in prayer and study.

What about concentration? Most people find themselves distracted when they pray alone. If it is possible, have you ever tried praying aloud rather than silently? Or writing out matters for prayer and going through them systematically? Perhaps best of all, is there someone else who is at one with you spiritually with whom you could pray? You could plan this for once a week to begin with—it is something that is more difficult to start than to stop if it's not working out!

Finally, one of the most general questions I have been asked about prayer was from a student who was new to the whole world of communing with God. 'How do you think about prayer generally?' he wondered, 'Is there a kind of illustration of what it means?' My first thought was to talk with him about the relationship of a father to his children, until I remembered that he had previously told me he had never known his father. So I tried another tack. 'You know how it is possible to use a hand mirror to catch the sun's rays, and deflect them upwards? If the mirror is angled in such a way, every ray that touches it can be deflected to the point you choose. I often think that the life of a believing Christian can so be angled upwards to God that everything that falls upon his life is deflected up to the throne of God either in thanksgiving and praise, or supplication and petition. If it is news of a need in someone else's life, that can be deflected to the throne in intercession.'

Perhaps more practically I have often found that concentration is helped when I take one of the psalms which is a prayer, and pray through the words of the psalm, if possible aloud. Examples of such psalms would be Psalm 23, Psalm 27, Psalm 40, Psalm 51, Psalm 63, Psalm 84, Psalm 86, Psalm 92, Psalm 96, Psalm 98, Psalm 100, Psalm 113, Psalm 121, Psalm 130, and the last six psalms are wonderful psalms of praise.

Of course your particular problem may not have been touched upon here, but whatever the problem, it is infinitely worthwhile to persevere in learning to pray.

# Epilogue:
## PRAYER AND PREACHING

RAYER AND PREACHING BELONG TOGETHER, and not just because of alliteration. They belong together in the mind and wisdom and purpose of God. Prayer is the *sine qua non* of preaching, because true preaching is not merely an intellectual or oratorical exercise, depending on human skills. It is a spiritual work, depending on the power of God to make his word living and effective, and the anointing of God, to make the preacher the vehicle of God's grace. That is why it is possible for someone to be brilliantly gifted as a scholar, an orator and a communicator, and yet, in the pulpit to be an irrelevance so far as God is concerned. The prayerless preacher is a contradiction in terms, as is the prayerless church. Dr Campbell Morgan, who preceded Dr Lloyd-Jones in Westminster Chapel, London, often told of a crisis in his ministry when he became aware that he was popular in the world but largely useless to God. It was as if God was saying to him, 'Preach on, great preacher—without me'. He went through a spiritual battle all that night, until in the morning he was bowed before God, acknowledging his absolute dependence on him.

It is this question which is at issue when we think of the relationship between prayer and preaching: where is my confidence? On what power do I ultimately depend? Do I covet a reputation more than the anointing of God on my ministry? Have I, also, allowed a division between prayer and preaching? It is never too late to put this right. Go now to God and confess your error to him, and then settle before him the God-given priority of ministry as in Acts 6:4, 'We will devote ourselves to prayer and to the ministry of the word'. Pray for prayer partners to be raised up to pray for you. If you do not yet have a prayer meeting in your own church, seek the help of other prayer meetings to pray for your preaching.

To church leaders who may read this, let me urge upon you the absolute necessity of a praying people for the preaching of God's word. You cannot separate prayer and preaching. A friend of mine (more bold than I!) once spoke with the leading layman in a church he was visiting. 'Do you have a prayer meeting?' he asked. The reply was, 'No we do not have such a meeting, but we have just invited a fine preacher to be our new minister'. My friend responded, 'If you do not have a prayer meeting in your church, you have no business inviting a minister into your pulpit'. Professor Finlayson of the Free Church College in Edinburgh was once asked, 'What is the greatest need of a young man entering his first ministry?'. His answer was, 'A praying people'.

It concerns me that in many evangelical churches which do have prayer meetings, the part of the work least prayed for is the preaching of the word on the Lord's day, and the one who has that responsibility. Paul pleads with the Church at Ephesus to pray for him, 'that utterance may be given to me, that I may open my mouth boldly to make known the mystery of the gospel'. May the church of Jesus Christ in our generation learn in depth how inseparable are prayer and preaching, and put what we learn into action.

### Teach Us To Pray

In mercy Lord, draw near,
Incline our hearts to pray.
O stir our souls to seek your face
And live by what you say.

Create  true thirst for you
An ardent, strong desire
To glorify your Holy Name.
And to your will aspire.

Lord, teach us how to pray,
Not just with lips alone.
Let heart and soul and mind and strength
Bring us before your throne.

Pour out your Spirit, Lord
Upon your Church  today,
Show us the Saviour's glorious work:
That new and living way.

Revive your cause O Lord,
The honour of your Name,
The glory of your only Son,
Who bore our utmost shame.

Grant us a childlike trust
In your sufficient grace.
Teach us to pray through all our days
Until we see your face.

*Eric J. Alexander*

*Also available from the Trust:*

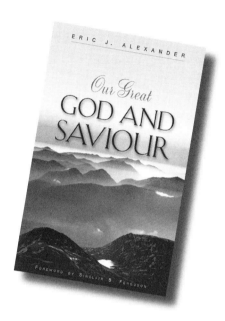

## Our Great God and Saviour

*Eric J. Alexander*

Those who sat under Eric Alexander's choice and fragrant ministry will hear the preacher's voice as they read this warm-hearted appreciation of the God he loves and adores. Echoes of Tozer, M'Cheyne and Lloyd-Jones resound at times as Eric guides us on a short but memorable journey through the Character, Salvation and Church of God. Simple yet profound, these sermons draw liberally on Christian poets of the past as well as pour forth meditations from the author's own heart.

[PEACE & TRUTH]

**ISBN: 978 1 84871 084 9  189pp  Paperback**

# About the Publisher

THE Banner of Truth Trust originated in 1957 in London. The founders believed that much of the best literature of historic Christianity had been allowed to fall into oblivion and that, under God, its recovery could well lead not only to a strengthening of the church today but to true revival.

Inter-denominational in vision, this publishing work is now international, and our lists include a number of contemporary authors along with classics from the past. The translation of these books into many languages is encouraged.

A monthly magazine, *The Banner of Truth*, is also published and further information will be gladly supplied by either of the offices below or from our website.

# THE BANNER OF TRUTH TRUST

3 Murrayfield Road
Edinburgh, EH12 6EL
UK

PO Box 621, Carlisle
Pennsylvania, 17013
USA

www.banneroftruth.co.uk